MW01002858

Laugh Tactics:
Master Conversational Humor and Be Funny on Command
Think Quickly on Your Feet

By Patrick King, Social Interaction Specialist at
www.PatrickKingConsulting.com

Table of Contents

Introduction

One of my favorite pastimes has always been watching standup comedy.

Originally, it wasn't even for the laughs and entertainment. I was interested because I had been trying to improve my public speaking skills and I wanted to study the presentation of the comedians. What were they doing to captivate audiences like they were, and in a way that business presenters and professors certainly weren't?

I started by intending to study their posture, body language, gestures, and manner of pacing, but I only lasted about five minutes before I was completely distracted and engrossed by what was happening on stage.

And that's when it struck me – being funny on command and making people laugh for an hour straight is one of the most difficult tasks in the world. What you're really doing is evoking an emotion whenever you want, at will. Movies and television shows spend millions trying to do that, and most of them still fail or can only do so in lukewarm ways.

People cry at movies sometimes, but not nearly as frequently as the producers and directors would want. And if the movie goes overboard, then suddenly it becomes cheesy and saccharine. Jokes in movies often fall flat, and even horror movies tend to rely on jump scares (a sudden noise or flash) rather than actual terror.

But comedians get on stage and make people laugh and guffaw for an hour straight, which is arguably one of the strongest emotions of all.

Impressive, right?

At first I thought it was purely talent-based and some people are just funnier than others. If there's a bell curve, there are obviously outliers. Some of us can run a mile in under seven minutes with no sweat, and others need an inhaler to walk up a short flight of stairs. We all have different predispositions.

But it wasn't until I investigated a little further and started reading about the comedy and joke writing process that I found that there were certain puns, premises, jokes, setups, and methods of delivery that were essentially *formulaic*.

Basically, there were patterns, steps, and even rules that even the most famous of comedians tended to follow – they had simply mastered them and could play with every type of variation instinctively.

Let's take a quick example - you may have noticed that comedians tend to talk about airports, sex, gender differences, and race.

That's because one of the rules that comedians follow is that their jokes have to be easily relatable and understandable – otherwise only about 10% of any given audience will be laughing. Therefore, they have to try to speak on universal themes and struggles.

There's no world in which I can claim to be a professional comedian, but by studying and breaking down exactly what the best in the world do to make people cry with laughter, I've found that there ways to be reliably, consistently, and constantly funny in conversation.

When you find the patterns and basic principles of what tends to make people laugh, you'll start to see jokes form before they even happen in front of your eyes. That's the best part – many of us feel like we struggle with normal conversation in general because it's so unpredictable. When something is unpredictable, it feels like we constantly have to adapt and think on our feet, and that's a scary proposition because it feels like it's only a matter of time before you slip up.

Laugh Tactics allows you to completely circumvent this feeling. When all you need to see is a pattern, a phrase, or a setup to have a joke immediately start to form in your head, you can say goodbye to the scariness of unpredictability.

Being a funnier conversationalist on a daily basis is equally about your mindset and approach, and just seeing life through a lens of play and humor versus a literal interpretation.

When someone asks you about their day, you can choose to answer literally, or you can make an observation about their jacket reminding you about Michael Jackson's jacket from the Thriller music video.

The goal for any type of change is to internalize it until it becomes a habit. I'm giving you step-by-step breakdowns to achieve this and become the charming and witty speaker you've always wanted to become.

Think fast!

Chapter 1. The Real Power of Being Funny

Visualize one of the worst days you've had at work in the past year.

What happened?

Maybe you broke the printer, you missed a crucial email, or you just came to work in a bad mood and alienated the entire office. On top of that, you just got a call from your landlord, and a water pipe burst in your home, flooding your bedroom. As a finale, there's a huge traffic jam, and you won't be able to get home for another three hours.

It's a bad day. It happens.

You decide to take a walk outside to clear your head, and you happen to see a dog refusing to walk, being literally dragged through the grass on a lease by his annoyed owner.

You can't help but laugh at the absurdity of it, which gives you a mental reprieve from your day and puts things into perspective. Your mood is instantly elevated and you take a picture to share with your friends.

That's the real power of humor. It allows us to get through our daily lives in the worst of times, and at the best of times, it allows us to be our best selves in front of other people.

Humor is an important part of our lives, and one of the primary emotions that drive us on a daily basis. It enhances many aspects of our lives, while also serving as an important coping mechanism to make other parts bearable.

It can immediately transform a bad day into a better day with some bad parts, as you can see from the example above.

Humor is great in getting through the tough times of life. Life is a series of valleys and peaks – if your life is a flat line, it's arguably worse and more tedious. No one worries when you're peaking, but when you're in a valley, such as if you lose your job, you have to find a way to cope and roll with the punches.

If that isn't bad enough, there is also the issue of our fears, our failures, and our hang-ups. A sense of humor, or the ability to create laughter, can diffuse the negative effect of the challenges we face and give us some perspective. It allows us to relax.

It can take interpersonal situations from tense and raw and make them tolerable. Humor enables us to diffuse these tensions, see the inherent silver lining and take things into perspective.

There are so many opportunities for tension and conflict in our lives. Even with people you know, there will be a situation where you rub them the wrong way, or they do the same to you. There's always the possibility that people mistake what you say or take your actions the wrong way.

Humor makes social interaction much easier. It lets people drop their guard and allow themselves to be comfortable with each other. Even if tension builds to a potentially explosive stage, a little bit of humor can diffuse what would have otherwise been a negative situation.

There's a reason that many successful standup comedians were late bloomers, or were picked on when they younger. They developed their sense of humor as defense mechanisms against those who laughed at them at their expense. They were able to being the butt of a joke into deflecting it to a collaborative joke. Humor lets people live their lives.

Aside from dealing with life's adversities, humor allows you to showcase the best sides of your personality – your cleverness, intellect, and wit.

We get to showcase what is so special about ourselves in a positive light, and what gives us value to others. Humor is amazing for this because we get instant, tangible, strong feedback in the form of simple laughter and smiles. We can make others feel good with humor. We make ourselves feel good because it draws attention to us in a positive way. It validates us, and makes us feel like part of a group and that we matter to the people around us. Many of us use humor as our primary form of validation.

Everybody craves some form of external validation, and anyone that says otherwise is lying through their teeth. Humor allows you to get that validation because it's an indirect way of showing off, and people typically assume intelligence in conjunction with witty, clever humor – minus fart jokes.

Indeed, it takes insight, seeing uncommon patterns, and creative thinking to be consistently funny. People recognize this.

In additional to intellect and wit, humor is a trait that is both consciously and subconsciously used for sexual selection.

According to research studies (separate studies by Jeffrey Hall and Nicolas Gueguen), males with better sense of humor are perceived as more sexually attractive by women. What makes this study interesting is that the perception of sexual attractiveness has nothing to do with how much money the man has, how much power he wields over other people, question of social status and social significance are also irrelevant, even good looks is not as important when a sense of humor is involved. A sense of humor can cut through normal expectations and elevate you instantly in the mind of the person perceiving you.

Even the most unattractive guy can draw positive attention from a very attractive woman by simply cracking the right joke at the right time.

If you think about the couples you know in real life, you'll realize that there may be some physical mismatches made logical simply because of one party's sense of humor and capacity for wit.

It's not overly surprising to see unattractive men with beautiful women on their arms. It may speak to the feelings of vulnerability and self-confidence that go hand in hand with a sense of humor.

Humor is the ultimate creator of social connections.

Humor is an excellent social lubricant. It allows you to identify and hang onto similarities and shared sensibilities. There is nothing more affirming than realizing that you and the person you are speaking to have the same sense of humor. You "get" each other. That sense of bonding and interpersonal chemistry is priceless and extremely rare.

Things that make you laugh consistently and predictably others may find flat, boring, and uninteresting. When you come across somebody that shares the same sense of humor, you can't help but feel a sense of affinity and similarity. You feel like you are on the same team.

This shared feeling can be a gateway to greater and deeper levels of mutual comfort. Humor, in this context, can make for a great springboard to more candid discussions. Humor also makes you feel more familiar and likeable to those who share your sense of humor. Even if they don't share your exact brand of humor, a sense of levity can go a long way in defusing natural skepticism or even downright suspicion.

Laughing hilariously over the same topics has been known to launch many a friendship solely on the basis that you are speaking each other's languages. Humor enables you to create a distinct bond based on what you find funny.

Finally, humor enables us to talk about things that are viewed as sensitive or off limits. I am talking about taboos. With the right application of humor, you can diffuse the tension surrounding these taboo topics. Humor can provide a gateway to frank and unfiltered discussions about things people would rather not talk about for either fear of offending others, or their own doubts on the subject in question.

Humor is simply one of the best emotions to feel, and thus be able to create.

It is the feeling of happiness, however momentary an interruption in people's days, that makes a difference. You can engage other people and take them into an entirely different, stress-free world. When you share an inside joke, you can instantly relate at a much deeper level, which makes for deeper relationships.

There is even a subconscious level of positive associations you may create because people associate you with feelings of joy, laughing, and humor.

Everyone has the capacity to be funny. Most people can manage to be funny from time to time. This book teaches you to go from being occasionally funny to being humorous and witty in a consistent manner. The more predictable your abilities, the more confident you become, and off to the races you go.

Chapter 2. The Unbreakable Rules of Comedic Delivery

In comedy, it doesn't really matter what you have to say.

What matters more, in most cases, is your delivery.

What exactly does this mean?

It makes little difference what you say. What makes it funny is *how* you say it, the timing, and the delivery. The actual words you use are important only to the degree that they were congruent with—and enhanced—the delivery.

Something similar happens when you examine verbal and non-verbal communication. Numerous studies have shown the amount of communication to be anywhere from 55% to 93% dependent on non-verbal cues. In other words, majority of human communication isn't with words, and we look for other signals to form the picture of humor.

One of the greatest tips in this book isn't something that I'm teaching. One of the best ways to be funnier is to expose yourself to humor and funny people on a daily basis. For most of us, the easiest way to do this is to watch standup comedy on YouTube and the like.

When you do this, try to take note of what the comedians are actually saying. You might be shocked that the statements by themselves aren't really that humorous or funny.

Taken out of context or in a vacuum, they might just sound like they are making an observation or an obvious statement. Try reading them out loud in a monotone voice. Is that going to make someone laugh? Probably not.

Let's do a little experiment to additionally showcase the importance of delivery.

Search for a video of your favorite comedian, whoever that may be. Personally, I've been entranced lately by Sebastian Maniscalco, an Italian-American comedian who is routinely shocked by the way people treat each other.

Make sure the video has closed captions or subtitles.

Turn the sound off and read the words out loud to

yourself. Try not to look at the facial expressions or gesticulations of the comedian. Just read the text as if you were reading from a book.

Objectively speaking, when you just read the printed text of what they have to say, they say nothing remarkable. It isn't really that humorous. There may be a few funny moments here and there that demonstrate some insight, but if you look at the cold text, you probably won't let out a belly laugh. You probably wouldn't even chuckle.

Now, reload that video and this time turn off closed captions and watch the video.

Turn on the sound and pay attention their gestures and how they move around the stage. How their body punctuates their sentences and how they modulate their voice to suit their jokes. It's the exact same material, but this time you are probably laughing out loud.

This experiment highlights the fact that being funny is all about delivery. This is good news. If you're like most people in this planet, you're probably not chock-full of humorous anecdotes and funny statements. Very few people are. You shouldn't worry about that, you only need to focus on how you deliver what you say to come off as a funny person.

Let's lay down some ground rules of what makes for great delivery, and what you should avoid.

Know Your Emotion

You need to be clear as to the emotion you want to evoke. It has to be articulable, and you have to know it beforehand.

If you don't have an emotion that you want to evoke from the other person, what are you even talking about, and what is the impact? It's probably going to be a story or anecdote that ends with people thinking "Oh... you're done now? That's the story?"

Knowing your primary emotion focuses your story or joke. It makes sure that it doesn't veer off into tangents and destroy your delivery. Even worse, people might not realize when you get to your punch line, or the part of the story that's supposed to be funny because you took such a winding road that no one could follow it.

"...And then we went surfing. Well, actually, it was body boarding, but some people say it counts as surfing so I'll go with that definition. Although, I did meet someone that said surfing is a proper term involving a certain sized board, so I don't know. Anyway, we went surfing..."

"... Was that it?"

That's not the kind of reaction you want. People who receive that kind of reaction did a lousy job in clarifying the emotional state they want to evoke from their audience.

The emotion you want to evoke from others is usually some variation of "Oh, that's funny," regardless if the story is positive or negative.

When you have this focus, you can actively think about what parts of your story are the funny parts, and what parts you should edit out in the name of getting to your punch line. You might exaggerate and add other parts that directly add to that one humorous punch line. Knowing your emotion gives you laser-like focus on what you are actually trying to do, and it will improve your storytelling skills regardless of the situation.

Deadpan, Smirk, or Grin

Now we move to the actual way that you deliver a story or joke.

I want to focus on three very different methods of delivery. It's helpful to know what makes each work so you can adapt them for your own purposes. These aren't the only methods of delivery, but they are among the easier ones to master.

The first step is to decide the tone of your story or joke. The tone determines which delivery method you will use.

If you want to convey dry humor, sarcasm, or disbelief, go with a deadpan delivery—that is, a serious tone and face.

"This toast is delicious." [If the toast is burnt to black crisp.]

"Good, we needed more fruit cake tonight." [If there are already four fruit cakes present]

If you want to convey something that you found was hilarious, or that is obviously humorous or absurd, go with the grin.

"Can you believe that we're matching from head to toe today?"

"Well, this night turned out like none of us expected!"

Finally, if you want to convey that something was amusing to you, but perhaps not inherently funny, or implying a double meaning, use a smirk.

"Oh, that's *exactly* what he meant."

"I don't know about you, but I don't see it."

The reason it is so important to properly use each is because if you don't use them properly, people won't know that you are joking, or at least not being serious, which can cause massive discomfort and actual tension.

However, it can also be part of the fun to create a momentary feeling of tension before breaking it by smiling, or making it very obvious you are joking. It's the contrast between the joke you are delivering and your serious demeanor that creates the perception of humor and gets people to laugh.

Your tone of voice is crucial in pulling this off. There are three very different tones to convey different feelings and emotions. It is important to know what these tones are and to make sure that it has the right effect.

Don't Backtrack

Backtracking is when you get bogged down in the details of the supposedly funny thing you were saying.

For example, when you over-explain it, go into tangents too much, continually correct yourself, or focus entirely too much on the details while ignoring the overall story, the joke is lost.

When you do this, it is painful for your audience. Remember, you are telling a story or joke for an emotional purpose that we defined earlier.

You may have people on the hook and a captive audience when you begin, but if you backtrack at all, their interest in your punch line will evaporate quickly. Remember, you're just trying to evoke one big emotion!

"So then we go skiing, right? Well, I almost got a snowboard but I decided I wanted to try skiing for the first time. My dad always loved skiing, so why not? So we go skiing – oh, I forgot to mention that I couldn't believe that my skis were purple..."

Zzzz.

You get so focused on the fine details of your funny story that when you backtrack you actually take away the impact of it. If that was a story about a ski collision, you've completely lost the plot and derailed the humorous buildup.

You come off like you are debating with yourself, and it ruins the comedic delivery.

It comes off like you really don't know what you're talking about, and people will be left grasping for the humor, assuming that is exists, in your story. Stay on point and don't dilute your message!

Spontaneity

Standup comics are practiced professionals.

They might seem quite sloppy, or relaxed and informal at times... but don't be fooled.

These people are not amateurs. They have gone

through years of haters and hecklers to fine-tune their craft. Some took drama classes, some did improvisation to hone their skills.

They have spent countless hours fine-tuning their delivery. Every stutter, groan, misstep, or self-interruption has been meticulously practiced and perfected to appear spontaneous. They understand the value of appearing spontaneous versus appearing rehearsed and wooden.

It's the difference between sounding like you are relaying a story to your friends versus giving a speech at a conference. It's a big difference.

But even if you are extremely rehearsed, don't let people know that.

You need to give people the impression that you're just speaking off the top of your head. Tell it like it's the first time you're telling it, or just thought of it at that moment. The alternative can be quite off-putting.

Humor is easier to understand and accept when people think you just came up with something out of the blue. Wit and cleverness are much more respected if they appear to be spontaneous, and thus highlights your creativity.

Never Laugh First

This one is simple. Don't be the first one to laugh at

your own joke.

You can laugh at your joke if you can't keep it in, but don't be the one that laughs before your audience, or before the punch line. It's a sign that you're insecure and you're not sure other people will laugh as well.

When you do this, you are essentially imposing your will on other people. And, most people like to appear nice, so they will laugh along with you. That's fine once or twice, and it might even work occasionally, but the laughs probably won't be genuine to start with.

Now, imagine someone doing that to you every five minutes. That's a whole lot of fake smiling and laughter, and it gets very obnoxious very quickly. You'll soon be branded as someone who has no self-awareness!

You're putting pressure on other people to *do something*, and that's not a feeling you want associated with you. It is exhausting and, at best, it is downright annoying.

As a final matter, it's a big flashing neon sign of insecurity and uncertainty in what you say. People who are sure of themselves and confident in their words don't laugh first because they know they speak value, and they don't care if you realize it or not.

One Sentence

Each story or joke should be able to be summarized in one sentence. If you can't do it, your joke or story lacks focus, or it doesn't have a point.

What happens when we aren't able to summarize ourselves in one sentence? We ramble like crazy.

It's because we try to find our story's purpose in a wandering and winding manner *while we tell it*. We go on tangents. Sometimes we find our purpose, sometimes not.

This has the same effect as backtracking. You lose any comedic effect you would have had otherwise, since people won't be paying attention to you anymore.

Rambling is a cardinal sin of storytelling, and it can be combated if you just think about summarizing yourself in one sentence first, then adding only the details pertinent to your big emotion and purpose afterwards, and filtering out those that don't.

When you focus on the point first, you are more likely to keep your joke short, snappy, and more effective. This maximizes its effect on the hearer.

Chapter 3. Creating a Mindset for Humor

In order to be a funnier conversationalist and have a better sense of humor in general, it's imperative to first fix your mindset.

Your current problem is probably that you are taking statements and questions from people at face value, not giving it a second thought, and staying in the literal track of a conversation.

Here's a quick and simple illustration. If I asked someone how the weather was outside, a literal, face value answer would be, "It just started to sprinkle. Looks cold"

An answer from someone who had a humorous mindset would be much different: "It's not wet enough to need an umbrella, but say goodbye to your hair-do."

As a social skills and conversation coach, conversations from my perspective are all about creating an enjoyable interaction. If you can make that your goal and accomplish it, then anything else you want to gain by talking to someone will flow naturally. Luckily, there are countless ways to reach an enjoyable interaction, and the humor mindset is one of the most prominent.

There's a reason that some people seem to have funny quips every minute, while you might feel like you have one good retort every two weeks. The difference isn't that they're inherently funnier, it's that they have the right mindset for it.

You may know what to do, but if you don't pair that with the right mindset, chances are, your jokes or banter will fall flat.

As you saw in the example above, most of us are stuck in the mode where we are too serious in our conversations. We think that just because they started a certain way, they need to fit a certain mold and follow that template or transcript to completion.

If someone asks about weather, yes, they want to know the temperature. But it doesn't stop there. You can answer the question in many ways that don't simply require you to answer it like a test question.

We have many expectations about where our conversations should go and how they should flow, but in reality, people don't care about these expectations.

This mindset often leads to conversations about things that neither party care about. What makes this so awkward is that both parties are just too polite to say anything about the conversation. No one wants to talk about the weather for more than one sentence each.

So, how can we create the mindset for us to instantly see more humor in our daily lives as a result of taking a different angle?

Playing Versus Discussing

This can also be called "Amusing Versus Conversing." There are many ways to look at these two different modes of thought.

The default conversation approach most people use is to, of course, discuss and converse. There's nothing wrong with that, and it can certainly lead to interesting revelations.

The problem is that it gets old quickly, and it can take on a serious and somber tone if that is your approach to a conversation. It's not the ideal way to build rapport since it can be a dry discussion of facts and news, which doesn't tell you anything about a person's personality, nor does it allow you to show your own off.

People discuss current events with colleagues. People play with and amuse friends with personal stories. See the difference?

The difference in mindset should be to focus on being more playful, not taking people at face value, and not worrying about answering questions literally. Just because they asked about the weather doesn't mean that you are only allowed to talk about the weather.

How can you do this?

You may actively think about how you react to someone in a playful manner. Imagine how you would react if you were five-years-old, and that is honestly a better approximation for playful conversation that can build rapport.

If someone asks you about the weather, what are the different ways you can reply?

You can ask silly questions, you can say things solely to see how others respond. You might create outlandish hypotheticals, you can address the elephant in the room, you can allow your inner monologue to be read out loud, and so on.

You may generally view the other person as someone to joke around with, as opposed to making a professional first impression on. You don't need to give people straight, exact answers. People are usually far more attracted to interesting and noteworthy answers. Unless you are giving an oral report, it's not a stretch to say that they would always prefer something to catch their attention versus be dry and accurate.

Remember that you're not necessarily looking to absorb a set of facts, or extract certain information. Instead, your goal is simply to feel good around those people and, most importantly, make them feel good around you.

Word of caution: be sure to actually answer someone's question. You can be both humorous and informative. Make sure to occasionally check in with the other person to make sure that you aren't going overboard with the lack of substantive content if they're seeking it.

Misconstrue Intentionally

Another method to prime your mindset for humor is to misconstrue what people say, but intentionally.

You're looking for opportunities for light misunderstanding, double entendre, puns, and comical confusion.

Usually, people try to police these and make sure they understand the other person as clearly as possible.

If you are trying to be humorous, you can do a

complete 180-degree turn. Instead of focusing on clear communication, you focus on these awkward phrases or potentially double-edged words that are exchanged. You use them as springboards to possible jokes. They can be gateways to humorous moments. Instead of spending so much time and effort running away from these, or quickly correcting them when they appear, use them as raw material for humorous moments.

Now that you have been introduced to intentional misconstruing, how would you respond to the following statements in a non-literal, deliberately incorrect way?

"I was so sore from the gym that I could barely take my shirt off."

"That is one huge cucumber."

"That's a jacket fit for eskimos."

Getting great at intentional misconstruing is a matter of practice and how you begin to see and hear things from other people.

Think Non-Linear

Usually, we imagine conversations to be structured in a very linear manner.

You start with Point A, you proceed to go through the

agenda of Point A and its subtopics, then you begin with Point B, and so on down the list. That works perfectly if you're in a boardroom going over a corporate agenda.

If you're trying to build rapport and have an enjoyable interaction, it pays off tremendously to think in non-linear terms. This means acknowledging Point A, while moving to Point B, then going straight to Point D, and looping back to Point A only at the end of the conversation.

That's the real winding path of a conversation. Relaxed, organic conversations are not very predictable, so you need to be able to adapt. Don't feel the need to stay on one topic, a related topic, or even an appropriate topic.

It is completely acceptable to transition from the weather to cars, to types of bread, to shopping for jeans. There doesn't have to be a transition between any two topics, and there doesn't need to be any transition when you want to bring back an older topic. That's a major sticking point some people have, simply because they feel like it might be awkward to suddenly bring up a new topic. But, is it awkward when you do it with your friends? It isn't, which means that this is an assumption based on social fear.

Make your conversation non-linear by simply talking about what you want. If you think about it this way, there is no way you can feel trapped in a topic. You are only trapped because you let yourself be.

By thinking about your conversations in non-linear terms, you take away a lot of its tendency to be dull, boring and "heavy." You can lighten things up by jumping from topic to subtopic and then back to the main topic again. This increases the likelihood that the other person would also be in an adventurous and playful mood.

In a roundabout manner, this means you shouldn't be going into conversations with agendas and overarching goals. If you stick to those agendas, you'll be trying to *force* conversations into linear thinking, and feel hopelessly lost when you deviate from that agenda.

What Would Sebastian Do?

If you want to be funny, it's a good idea to study people that make their living being funny. Professional comedians can teach you volumes about delivery and finding openings and opportunities. You also get a tremendous array of potential humor role models.

As of the time of writing this book, Sebastian Maniscalco is my favorite comedian.

He's funny, but he also has well-defined personality traits. He's cranky, critical, observant, petty, easily annoyed, grumpy, and easily indignant.

Having that list of adjectives makes it pretty easy for me to simply ask, "What would Sebastian do in this situation?" or, "How might Sebastian respond here?"

You can start looking at situations based on their perspective. By simply assuming their perspective, you're more able to find the humor in certain topics that you used to think were so serious. You're able to step out of your mindset and into someone else's.

Humor is a point of view, and you are using another person's.

Suppose it is Halloween night, and you are wearing a vampire costume. It's pretty easy to imagine how you might play that role, right? Having a comedic role model does the same for you, and makes it easy when you run out of things or say, or your mind blanks.

You can step into their shoes and look at situations in a novel way, and at the very least, you can find more options in how to approach humorous situations. If I can imagine what Sebastian would say, then I won't have a blank mind or run out of things to say.

Think Slightly Inappropriate

This is a mindset that you should act carefully on, and only when you are sure of yourself.

It's predicated on the fact that when you talk about "appropriate topics," they usually turn out to be boring and shallow. There are only so many interesting things you can say about work, the weather, grocery shopping, and ice skating. We stay on these topics because we feel like anything more and we are invading people's privacy and secrets. It's not true, but it's a mental barrier we place on ourselves to err on the side of caution, not realizing that the window of appropriateness continues to shrink.

That means to have better, funnier conversations, you need to skew to the slightly inappropriate.

What do you speak about to your close friends? I'd bet you don't stick to appropriate and professional topics. Inappropriateness gets people talking and laughing, and almost no one is ever offended by it. There is a limit you may have put on yourself to keep things appropriate, and that unfortunately keeps you conversationally vanilla, and your relationships remain cold and distant because people don't think they can open up to you beyond a certain level.

You can do this in two ways.

The first way is to have a slightly inappropriate take on a boring topic.

"Ice skating? I just saw this YouTube clip where someone's ear was sliced off from a skate!"

The second way is to bring up a slightly inappropriate

topic by itself.

"Yeah, ice skating is fun. I think I only like figure skating because of the tiny leotards the women wear, though."

When you introduce something slightly inappropriate (slightly being subjective), you become the substitute teacher who swears in the first minute. Students never know what kind of teacher the substitute will be, so when they swear, everyone sighs with relief because they know the substitute is relaxed and not draconian.

When you get people laughing and relaxed around you, this gives you the opening to establish rapport.

When you break the boredom with inappropriateness, you're doing them a favor by going beyond the conventional and predictable.

Chapter 4. Common Mistakes in Jokes and Humor

Up to this point in the book, I've given you some tips for humor and to make sure that you aren't a humor vampire, meaning that you suck the humor out of the room.

I would hope that you've already learned some tactics that allow you to be more humorous, and that you've tried them out and found some success!

However, it's important to recalibrate at this point, and that's why this is such an important chapter.

You may have found some initial success, but you may also have bad habits from before that can impede your progress to be funnier and wittier.

The greater factor that truly makes or breaks your success is your attitude. You should have an intellectually curious and adventurous attitude.

Nothing should be sacred to you, but at the same time, you should respect people's sensitivities. I know it's a little bit of a tightrope here, but truly great conversationalists are not only able to walk this tightrope, they master it. They produce predictable results time and time again.

With that said, keep in mind the following common mistakes. If you completely overlook these, or don't pay enough attention to them, they can rob some of the power of your attempts at humor.

Consider this a good starting point for the "don't do" list on being funny.

Being Generic

This one is common sense.

If you're going to crack a joke, make sure that it's a joke that the other person hasn't heard countless times, or if they had, you take an unexpected or unusual spin on it.

If the joke is too generic and people have heard it before, even just the sentiment, people won't find you funny. They might chuckle in slight amusement, but they might develop a negative judgment of your sense of humor because it's so predictable and generic. They might walk away with a conclusion that you're a fairly generic person with nothing unique to say.

This requires you to analyze whether your joke is generic and something people have heard before. For instance, someone with red hair has heard countless times about being a "ginger," and store clerks will hear countless times that since something didn't scan, it must be free.

If you've heard a joke before, chances are, the person you're speaking with has also heard it before. Similarly, if you have used the joke before, try not to use it again. It's not worth repeating to the same people.

Always try to add something new to it, or twist it to produce a different perspective. It's perfectly okay to recite old jokes, but you need to put a distinct twist to it. Don't stick to the low hanging fruit, which are the obvious paths to humor that everyone will have seen or heard already.

If you do this properly, people will understand what you did. People will get an appreciation for your creativity. You've taken something that is fairly old and familiar and, through your creativity and imagination, put a distinct twist to it that is very welcome indeed.

Picking the Wrong Audience

You must have a feel for your audience.

Different people have different backgrounds. We have

a wide variety of experiences, educational attainments, class backgrounds, and so on.

What may be funny with one particular social circle might not be so funny, or even make sense, to other social circles. Sometimes people might even find what you said flat out insulting or offensive.

You have to make sure you have a somewhat clear understanding of the audience you're in front of. If you don't, at best they simply won't get the joke. At worst, they might be offended at what you had to say.

If you're speaking to kids about expensive Louis Vuitton handbags, they lack the context to understand it. If you talk to people at a homeless shelter about those bags, you might be outright offensive by pointing out their situation in life.

In this way, you proactively think of humor from other people's perspectives. This is good practice for any type of conversation. You develop a sense of boundaries and context for why people say the things they do. You ensure that you speak people's languages and talk about matters they can understand and relate to.

You'll also begin to understand why the same "offensive joke," when spoken by somebody who is perceived to be a member of the group, is welcomed. But when told by an outsider, they might think, "What gave you the right to crack that joke? I don't know or trust you enough to give you permission to say that joke to me."

Knowing your audience can be boiled down to calibrating your humor to other people, not the other way around or assuming that humor is universal.

Rushing the Punch line

Another common mistake among would-be funny people is rushing the punch line.

They are so excited about the value of the joke and look forward so much to making the other person laugh that they either rush *to* the punch line, or *through* the punch line. Sometimes they can barely contain themselves and giggle all the way through it. It all depends on what you are trying to convey. If you are trying to convey that you were so entertained that you couldn't contain yourself, that's fine from time to time.

If you are trying to make someone *else* laugh, it's not ideal.

In many cases, people rush through the whole joke or story, skimping on necessary details or completely destroying the sense of buildup. This is a problem, because great jokes, as I've mentioned, are great not because of their inherent content but because of their delivery.

If you were to just rush to the punch line or rush through the bulk of the joke, you destroy your timing and your delivery.

While the content of the joke is preserved, the impact of the joke was severely compromised. You've gone through the process of setting up the joke and delivering the punch line all for nothing.

Take your time. Pay attention to the feedback you get and properly time the punch line. Make sure you set up your audience each step of the way, otherwise, your punch line simply won't have much of an impact. In a sense, you just need to hit your marks.

Realize that a natural tendency for public speaking is to speak quickly due to the inherent adrenaline rush. Humor is not so different in this aspect.

Overlooking Delivery

Go back and re-read the prior chapter on comedic delivery.

Delivery is crucial. You don't want to come off like you're rambling or lost, and you don't want to overcorrect.

It's important to be clear about the main emotion you want to create in the person you're speaking with.

Avoid the tendency to laugh first to plant the seeds of

laughter for other people.

Watch video clips of comedians and study them.

One more thing that wasn't mentioned previously: when you express an emotion like happiness or sadness, can people tell? In other words, are you able to convey what you're thinking effectively, or do you need work on making your emotions more plain and obvious to punctuate your stories and jokes?

Leaving Out Vital Information

On some level, conscious or subconscious, jokes have a logical flow.

There's some level of thinking involved, and everything from the setup to the premise to the punch line makes it funny. They all work in tandem, and guess what? The entire effect is lost if one of those elements is missing.

At best, your punch line is going to be as funny as you intended it to be. At worst, your joke will leave people saying, *"And then what happened? Oh... is that it?"*

This step is easy. Get into the habit of performing self-edits and checking in with yourself when you want to talk about something humorous. Sometimes we rush, or something gets lost in translation between our minds and our mouths.

Try to actually analyze the action, the premise, and the punch line: what the three elements are and what you can definitely *not* leave out in order for people to understand your point. What are the actual points that matter and make the joke work? It might not be what you think, and you might emphasize the wrong thing if you don't examine yourself.

This point is as much about being thorough as it is about self-analysis, and making sure you adhere to a logical flow.

Not Tracking People's Reactions

You have to be able to read people!

Just because you think something is funny doesn't mean anyone else does.

Truly great comedians are great precisely because they are able to bounce signals back and forth with their audience members. They read the audience and this impacts what they say, how they say it, as well as their overall timing.

While you are telling your joke or story, or using humor in general, you have to pay attention to the other person to read their reaction. Try not to get lost in the moment and in the telling of your story or joke. Essentially, if you are getting a good reaction, keep doing what you are doing. If not, change it up.

Study their faces and try to gauge their reactions. Think about whether they are enjoying what you're saying. Pay attention to how they react, and modulate what you say based on content, delivery and tone.

Don't become "that girl" or "that guy" in the room who people avoid because they lack the ability to track people's reactions, and lack the self-awareness to realize that they might not be funny.

One of the easiest ways to do this is to examine their smiles, and you can dissect people's smiles in three ways.

First, fake smiles fade quickly.

When someone has a genuine smile, it is brought on by an emotion, not by a conscious decision. This means the genuine smile takes some time to fade, and remains after the punch line. If someone's smile instantly fades when they speak, or by the time you're on your next sentence, it's fake and they were pandering to you to some degree.

Second, fake smiles don't show teeth.

Genuine smiles are when the facial muscles pull apart and the teeth are revealed. If someone gives you a tight-lipped, toothless smile, it's a dead giveaway that they are manufacturing a smile for you. It's not brought on by emotion, and it's voluntary.

If someone's habit is to smile with their teeth closed, or they are self-conscious about their teeth or mouth, you can tell they are really smiling because they are trying to force their lips together, or they cover their mouth when they smile or laugh.

Third, fake smiles have wide eyes.

Real smiles are involuntary and are essentially facial spasms in reaction to emotions. A real smile will have crinkles around the eyes, and the eyes will appear slightly squinted because the ocular muscles will be affected. If the eyes are wide open, they aren't feeling something genuine, and they're putting on a show for you.

Chapter 5. The Humor of Relatability

One of the greatest interpersonal and comedic pleasures is when you crack a joke about a subject, and someone that you thought had zero interest in that subject laughs their head off.

A primary aspect of humor is being able to share your feelings with someone and find that you are both on the same page. You might have the same thoughts as they do about electric cars, or you both might hate the same types of yoga. Either way, humor is a strong emotion, and it creates a strong feeling of connection.

Whatever it is, humor opens people up to find commonalities that create real bonds. You can use humor to realize all of your shared experiences, and how much you can relate to each other.

We live in a world filled with perceived social distances, and it's easy to feel like you're drifting through many different social spaces completely alone. It's easy to feel alienated and disconnected. When a well-timed joke lands with someone else, we realize other people can relate to topics, situations, and issues like we do, and this sense of isolation or alienation disappears for a bit.

Relatability is a powerful humor tactic. It taps into our innate human need to belong to something greater than us. We float through life feeling like we're doing it alone and in an isolated way.

Relatability is *hilarious* because of the shock involved in discovering that something you thought only you knew or had experienced is shared in a big way.

The subject matter is not necessarily what's important. The humor is in the fact that you and that person share a perspective.

For example, everyone has experienced burning the roof of their mouth with hot pizza because they were too hungry or impatient to wait for the pizza to cool off.

If you were to bring this up, it's going to be funny because it happened to them in the past as well. The key here is to come up with an experience that is universally relatable.

In the case of hot pizza, your joke is funny since most people can relate to that. Most people have rushed through eating something hot and burned the roof of their mouth, but it's not something we discuss at length, if at all. But by mentioning it, you shine a light on it and make the experience shared – something that people didn't know other people hated is brought into the open.

Let's make a list of other things people hate.

1. Bread crumbs in jam or butter.

2. That moment when you're walking towards someone but unsure of when to make eye contact.

3. The awkward feeling when you say goodbye to someone and then proceed to walk in the same direction.

4. Honking angrily at someone in your car and then pulling up next to them at a stoplight.

5. When you start the chain reaction of a set of dominoes, but it stops halfway through.

These are inherently funny because everyone can relate to the feelings involved. You have called out an invisible elephant in the room and made it comfortable for people to agree and shout, "Hey, me too!" This is additionally funny because you've taken the time to articulate this feeling that everyone is familiar with.

If you think about everyday things that annoy you, chances are high that they annoy other people, too.

To use relatability humor, come up with something that is nearly universal. It doesn't matter what country that person comes from, what religion they belong to, how much education they have or how much money they make. The more general or universal the experience, the funnier your joke will be, and the more people will find it funny.

There's a reason standup comedians seem to talk about sex, gender, airports, children, and eating a lot. It's because they are universal topics that everyone can relate to. Most other topics are too niche, too opinion-based, or too complex and multi-faceted.

Stay universally relatable and you can cut through everything that divides us, and unite people through a shared experience. People like to feel that you "get them" and you understand them on a deeper level.

Step one: find something small that annoys you on a daily basis.

The smaller and more insignificant, the better.

You can't talk about a topic that is big, like government corruption, because there are simply too many shades of gray and too many opinions attached to it. It's big and complicated. The smaller it is, the better.

Burning the roof of your mouth with pizza, bread crumbs in jam, locking yourself out of your apartment, and not being able to take all of the grocery bags in one trip are universal, small annoyances of everyday life. I challenge you to find someone who doesn't have a visceral reaction to those things.

If you have trouble with this, try visualizing your day, right from the moment you wake up to the moment your head hits the pillow at night. Walk through your day and all the actions that you perform. What are your small annoyances and pet peeves?

Here are some examples of the morning annoyances you can list: waking up with a pillow full of drool, having breath that makes you feel like a bug died in your mouth, getting white toothpaste on your black slacks, and so on.

Step two: exaggerate in a vivid way how much pain that small thing caused you.

For example, burning the roof of your mouth with pizza is like setting your gums on fire or pouring acid on them.

Getting toothpaste on your black slacks is like being the only one in the office to wear a Halloween costume.

Thinking about calling in sick to work because you spent entire geological eons looking for your keys, when they were on the hook where you usually keep them in the first place.

Step three: connect the two.

You can say, "I really hate it when pizza burns the roof of my mouth, this pepperoni pizza was like taking a bite into delicious acid."

Or, for example, "I hate getting toothpaste on my pants, I feel like I'm the one person who didn't get the memo that we don't wear costumes during Halloween."

When you exaggerate, you draw parallels and an analogy to something that people can relate to. You come off as funny because you're referring to things that they have experienced in an exaggerated and vivid way.

Here's another example: "I hate building Ikea furniture." The exaggerated version is, "Ikea furniture is like a puzzle that's missing twenty pieces at the beginning."

The objective of the relatability approach is to show that you have shared experiences, and you can process and analyze them on a deeper level. The usage of comparison and analogy is another component of humor here.

Step four: use it.

The way you use it isn't when you're building furniture, it's any other context you want to show displeasure, "I was more miserable during that race than when I had to build my Ikea desk. It was like a puzzle missing twenty pieces."

For example, "That meeting was so agonizing, I'd rather take a bite of hot pizza and burn my mouth with that delicious acid."

You have essentially prepared these funny, relatable jokes beforehand, and now you can pepper them into your speaking to be more colorful, witty, and funny at the appropriate time.

You also show people how in tune you are and how you can connect concepts.

With a few well-placed jokes, you can reveal something about yourself to the people around you. When they realize that you're not that different from them, it becomes much easier for them to open up. People see themselves in your reactions, and all because you acknowledge the little things we are all annoyed with on a daily basis.

Chapter 6. Emphasizing Contrast

One of my favorite movies of all time is the movie *Elf*, starring Will Ferrell.

I'm a Will Ferrell fan in general, but I think this movie stands heads and shoulders above all others because of the premise and the comedy that flows naturally from the stage that is set.

The overall premise is that Will Ferrell's character, Buddy, is a human child who has somehow been adopted by the elves of Santa's workshop.

Elves are munchkin-sized, and even human children dwarf an adult elf. (That was a very mythical sentence.)

When Buddy is a child, he is roughly the same size as his adopted Elf parents. As soon as he hits puberty and exceeds three feet in height, he becomes a giant in the workshop. Very soon, nothing fits him and everything has to be custom-built.

You can imagine the kinds of dilemmas that occur with even the simplest of daily tasks. Showering, using the toilet, and using any mode of transportation have to be completely re-thought because nothing was designed for Buddy's size and shape.

It's just like if a sentient shark started living in your home. Nothing would work for them except for the bathtub.

The movie *Elf* is a wonderful example of **emphasizing a contrast**. You take two things that could never go together, or that take ingenuity to fit together, and then see how the chips fall. The chips typically fall in hilarious ways because you try to reconcile two opposing concepts, which is usually impossible under normal circumstances.

Set them up next to each other and point out what makes them different from each other. The humor is in seeing or feeling just how far removed or different they are, and then imagining all of the "fish out of water" situations that brought you to that point, or that will occur in the future.

You're treated to a battle of wits, values, and will.

Elf did this by putting a literal giant beside tiny elves and experimenting with the interplay of that size difference. There's nothing quite like seeing Will Ferrell try to shower with a showerhead that only goes up to his belly button.

Emphasizing contrast doesn't have to be that drastic. In daily life, it's just a matter of being more observant and calling out a situation that doesn't really fit together, or that a situation is fortuitous and circuitous when you think about it more closely.

It can be as simple as to point out, *"Okay, so I'm a Minnesota farm boy that didn't have electricity growing up and here I am at a technology conference. Wild, huh?"*

A strong contrast creates a rich environment for unexpected punch lines to appear and essentially takes advantage of the element of surprise.

Things become funny when situations that normally produce a predictable outcome don't, and in fact that outcome is something extremely different.

One way to phrase this situation is that emphasizing contrasts *defies expectations*.

When people look at a situation and create a narrative to surround it, their brains automatically look for the tried and proven path. We don't even think about it, it kicks in naturally and we expect what we have seen before. If you're a Minnesota farm boy, you're not expected to be a software programmer who owns four iPads.

Now, when you short circuit this and you take away a notion and replace it with something that flies in the face of the expected result, this is a tremendous opportunity for something funny.

If you see someone who is seven feet tall and athletic, you might wonder if he played basketball. Your expectations are defied if you discovered that he instead was a champion jump-roper or had never played basketball in his life.

For another example of pointing out inherent contrasts, one could say "I really like camping and almost never comb my hair, and here I am at a nail salon getting a manicure."

Usually a person who likes the great outdoors doesn't care about getting a manicure. Chances are, their knuckles and fingernails are ragged and dirty. In many cases, they really couldn't care less about what other people thought about them or their appearance.

When somebody says the sentence above, it creates a contrast between what the person is normally like and the person's activity at that moment. We get something that we didn't expect. We were thrown a curveball. You take a notion one way, then end with it the complete opposite.

You also create interesting imagery when you emphasize contrasts and put them next to each other.

Similarly, the statement "I'm six-foot-five and two hundred fifty pounds, but I have to tell you, I really enjoy sewing and needlepoint. It's my guilty pleasure."

The contrast here is between the size of the person and our normal expectations of someone with that physique, and what that person's actually into.

Usually, when somebody is that magnitude in size, this type is expected to be into football, rugby, or any sort of highly physical sport, but it turns out that the speaker is into sewing – the stereotypical activity of grandmothers killing time on a slow Sunday afternoon.

You don't need a certain type of size or strength to sew or crochet. In short, the person sets up a contrast between his expected physical interests, and his actual interests which are more crafts-related.

If you've watched the movie *The Tooth Fairy* starring Dwayne "The Rock" Johnson, you can see another example of how contrast humor works.

It's all about defying expectations. You look at The Rock's physique and perceived interests and they normally have nothing to do with being a tooth fairy:

someone who has wings, wears a tutu, and has the word "fairy" in his name.

The humor springs from the direct inconsistency of our expectation with what the subject actually says.

This is the underlying structure of most romantic comedies and buddy cop movies.

Two people are working together, or falling in love, and if they were similar and got along fabulously, it wouldn't make for a very interesting movie.

Instead, you take two people that have completely different expectations and come from different sets of circumstances, and you explore that interplay.

Take the movie series *Rush Hour* with Jackie Chan and Chris Tucker. The movie's running gag is that it pairs two very different people with very different temperaments together and puts them in outlandish situations. The humor springs from their contrasting reactions to each other's cultural norms, and how they adapt differently to the same situation.

How can you use this more in your daily life?

Of course, we don't have the benefit of setting up circumstances that will automatically yield big contrasts. The way to use them more in your daily life is to observe more and realize that plenty of funny contrasts already exist around you. All you have to do is boil people down to a few specific traits and characteristics for the sake of humor.

Think of your best friend. What kinds of stereotypes do they fulfill? Would you call them a jock, a nerd, a tech geek, a wild child, a rebel, a hippie, a worrier, a leader, a control freak? Feel free to over-generalize and shoot from the hip. Don't overthink this.

You can base this on their rough physical appearance, their occupation, or their basic personality traits. Don't get specific, otherwise you'll find it hard to stereotype or categorize them.

This is the first step.

As soon as you have a few of their stereotypes down and you can label them in just a few words, it's time to hunker down and think about how they defy those stereotypes. Do you have a friend who is incredibly clean and is a neat freak, but they volunteered to plan the company food fight? Maybe your friend was valedictorian of her college engineering class, but is now a hippie farmer?

What kind of contrasts can you find within that one person, and in what ways do they defy expectations that would otherwise flow from the stereotype?

The downside to this type of humor is that it can easily become mechanical and predictable.

Predictability is the antithesis of contrast comedy. Contrast comedy is no longer funny if you can see what will happen next.

Most people appreciate wit and intelligence. Unfortunately, many people go about showcasing these two personality traits in the worst way possible. Contrast humor enables you to show off your humor without coming off as hogging the spotlight, or even directly drawing attention to yourself. All you are doing is drawing contrasts and connecting the dots, which make people laugh while giving the impression of intelligence. Good deal!

Chapter 7. False Importance

As you may have noticed with the previous chapter, emphasizing contrast and the natural humor that creates, and breaking and defying expectations is a cornerstone of humor.

There are endless opportunities for humor when there is a surprise difference between what is expected and what actually occurs.

This chapter uses the same basic principle. The false importance tactic draws from the same reservoir of humor.

In a nutshell, with false importance you take small and petty matters (the smaller and pettier the better) and react with inflated importance and emotion to them.

Similarly to the last chapter, you defy expectations and create an incongruity in people's minds. They expect a small reaction to a small and petty issue, but they receive the polar opposite. It takes them by surprise and makes them laugh from the juxtaposition.

You create a contrast between something normal and something absurd, except this time, you're on the side that is being more absurd.

The final aspect to false importance is that you create a slight moment of intense tension. For a heartbeat, people aren't sure if you are serious about your outrage or whether you're kidding. When it becomes obvious that you are kidding, either because the situation is that absurd, or you break into a smile, part of the laughter will stem from that release of tension.

Like most laugh tactics, explanations don't do this justice. They are best seen through illustration and feel.

What are some ways that you can use the false importance tactic and make mountains out of molehills in a joking way?

False Importance #1

Let's start with the easiest one: making a big deal out of something small and displaying the corresponding *rage or triumph*. Something tiny has happened, and you are going to display an immense emotion. It doesn't have to be an inherently positive or negative action.

By taking something small and drawing a huge exaggerated conclusion, you can create both a funny situation, and amusement based on tension release.

You can make a big deal out of something small happening or not happening. You can become extremely happy or extremely angry at something small happening or not happening.

"This is TAP WATER? Do you know who I am?!"

"You have TEN pens there? You sicken me."

"Is your watch from Timex? I hate you."

"Is your watch from Timex? Gosh, stop showing off."

Other examples include calling yourself a big deal when you get a plastic toy with your drive-thru meal, or incredible rage that you only got one ketchup packet.

You can become extremely happy or extremely angry based on something someone does or says.

"I can't believe you parked there. It's SO FAR." [When the parking spot is 10 feet away from the front door.]

"You bought three pairs? This is the best day of my life!"

The delivery is important when you use the false importance tactic.

Do your best to sound serious. Stay in character. Don't use a sarcastic tone, and say it like you truly believe it. If you use a sarcastic tone, then counter-intuitively you may sound like you're being passive aggressive. That leads to people feeling offended, becoming guarded around you, and ultimately avoiding you. Not the best use of humor.

Make sure to break character in some way, perhaps by giving a sly smile, so people know that you are indeed kidding. Express the emotion genuinely, then break!

False Importance #2

Another way to impart false importance is to misconstrue something tiny to be a huge, exaggerated deal.

This isn't about emotions like the last iteration of this tactic. This is about consequences and rewards. Take an inconsequential act, and assume that it will lead to riches and a privileged life or a downfall into homelessness.

For example, *"Yeah, we found parking five feet away from the front door. We're royalty tonight."*

Or, *"I got this watch on sale for ten bucks. When do we start filming my rap video?"*

Or, *"Yes, I got fewer fries than you. That proves my theory that all women just hate me. Leave me alone!"*

False Importance #3

You can impart false importance by using official terms for silly and small things.

When you use terms that are usually reserved for professional and managerial purposes in casual or inappropriate contexts, you create a pleasing defiance of expectation.

For example, using management buzzwords and using it when you describe a drinking contest, or analyzing a Disney movie using economics theories.

"Now, when she drinks that beer, she's going to rank in the top quartile of all alcoholics. I looked at my ALC-1 report and the probability is very likely."

"I'd love to work for that company! They believe in equality, in a 'Jungle Book' sort of way."

False Importance #4

This deals with false insults and compliments. This is when you construe anything that people say as either a high compliment, or a subtle and passive aggressive (or downright aggressive) insult.

This one is easy.

"Are you going to finish that piece of pie?" "Are you calling me fat (or skinny)? I resent that."

"That's a nice shirt." "I get it. My other shirts are terrible."

"Is that a new watch?" "I know, my taste is amazing. I can go shopping with you if you want next time."

Again, delivery is imperative. First, say it like you believe it and stay in character, otherwise the entire effect will dissipate. Only then you can break and give a sly smile.

It's about creating contrast. Take something that has its own range of expectations and put a twist to it so that those expectations are overturned.

The great comedian Steve Allen used to do this regularly with pop music songs. He would take the most mundane and extremely forgettable piece of some one-hit wonder and recite the lines with extreme solemnity and seriousness. He would make dramatic pauses and then resume with a lot of emotional gravity and pathos in his voice.

He would often stop and feign shock and even outrage at the audience's reaction. What he was really doing was drawing attention to just how absurd the lyrics were and creating a contrast between absurd lyrics and Shakespearian delivery.

Remember, create a contrast and people will love the unexpected surprise. It shakes them a little out of their comfort zone, and instantly calls attention to you.

Chapter 8. Vivid and Outlandish Imagery

If there's a theme I would hope that you've learned thus far from this book, it's that to be funny, you don't always need to actively attempt to be funny like a stand-up comedian.

If you constantly try to crack jokes, make connections, and set up punch lines, chances are that you're probably going to be more obnoxious than funny. As we've seen from previous chapters, not all humor is like that.

This *book* is focused on making your personality funnier naturally, in addition to giving you some ways to create humorous setups. This *chapter* straddles both.

Take the difference between someone that happens to have flaming red shoes and whose favorite shirt has cartoon zebras fighting. He's not trying to be funny, he just has a disposition and approach to life that might be more conducive to being naturally funny. He would describe a pie in terms of deliciousness versus flavor.

To be funny, you don't have to intentionally try. You can use vivid and outlandish imagery to describe what you see and make analogies.

You're reading this book in English, and in the English language, there are words that are superior to others for comic effect.

You could say that someone is "funny," but you could also say that they "made your cheeks ache from laughing."

We use lazy, uninspired language on a daily basis, and part of being funnier is to slowly replace those common terms and phrases with more flavorful ones.

You could call someone "stupid," but you could also call them a "buffoon" or "nincompoop" – objectively rarer and sillier words, and less directly insulting than "stupid".

Other examples of words that are inherently funny, or at least unusual, are:

- Lake Titicaca (a real lake)
- Dingleberry
- Discombobulate

- Blubber
- Poppycock
- Gobbledygook

Not that you should be using those words specifically, but there is definitely a range of more creative words you can be using. The first step here is to realize that we naturally speak in a boring and overly-sanitized manner.

Our vocabulary and daily sense of imagery is sorely lacking, and we need to fix that to become more interesting and funny with unnoticeable effort. Remember in your English (or SAT) classes when you learned new vocabulary– the ones with four or five syllables?

You'd pepper them into your vocabulary subtly to make yourself sound intelligent and erudite. See? I just did it myself.

If you commit to replacing parts of your vocabulary, and thinking for a split second more when you describe things, these small changes can make a big difference as to how you are perceived.

Someone who "dances funny" is barely a blip on our screen, but someone who "dances like a gorilla cooking an omelet" catches our attention immediately.

Usage #1

The first step is to destroy normal adjectives from your vocabulary and replace them with something that you have to think about. Other people often will not have actively thought about it, and it will be unexpected.

If you wanted to say that your weekend was "good," what might be better and more descriptive ways of doing that?

Good -> imaginative -> splendid -> like a big Bloody Mary -> better than using the bathroom after a long car ride -> almost as good as Christmas morning.

If you wanted to say that you love coffee, what might be a better and more descriptive way of doing that?

I love coffee -> it is my lifeblood -> I'm dead without it -> my blood is fifty percent caffeine -> I would bathe in it if I could -> I drink so much my urine looks like coffee too.

See the difference?

It's not difficult, but it's not easy to come up with on the fly, either. This is a mindset you have to proactively cultivate. Whenever you come across a normal adjective, think of what other synonyms you might use in giving people descriptive answers.

When you use better words and phrases, you'll make people react to them because you are saying much more than just the words and phrases themselves.

Usage #2

Another way to inject vivid and outlandish imagery into your daily speaking is to simply choose to describe observations, actions, and objects in an unconventional and creative way.

For example, comedienne Amy Schumer has a great example of this when she describes her sleeping positions. She *could* describe how she sleeps as "messy" or "weird." She could even go another level up and say she sleeps like an "unsalted pretzel."

The unsalted pretzel gives you a mental image, but she does even better.

She describes her sleeping position to be "as if she fell from the top of a building" or "in the shape of a swastika."

There's your instant mental image, which now has the added intelligent humor of combining two very different concepts (sleep and swastika, sleep and falling off of a building).

Another example of this is from PJ O'Rourke, who described his experiences with local military in the

Philippines, involving contact with a small policeman that amazed him.

He described the policeman as very intimidating and scary, but also very petite. His exact phrasing was, "he looked like an attack hamster."

Even if you're not trying to be funny, just the way you come up with analogies on how you contrast and compare different concepts can make for really funny descriptions.

How do you master the art of humorous descriptions?

The first step is to attempt to disassociate from what you see, and just focus on the elements and traits of what you see.

For example, in the case of PJ O'Rourke, you would disassociate that you were looking at a police officer, and focus on the elements and traits of the police officer.

He was small, petite, scary, intimidating, powerful, fierce, authoritative, serious, severe, and elfin.

What are two distinct concepts that would fit the descriptions above?

O'Rourke identified a small animal, a hamster, and also played on the fact that this person had a strong physical and military capability who can attack. When you put those two concepts together you may come up with the funny image of an attack hamster.

This type of humor really stretches your imagination and creativity. You're forced to brainstorm what the basic elements are related to, and what they resemble in a physical level. These weird combinations create funny images like Amy Schumer's description of sleeping.

Another great benefit about this particular approach to humor is that it necessarily increases your vocabulary. It also exercises your creative thinking in coming up with weird analogies and weird connections on the fly. Compare this with simply saying the same words over and over again like "good" and "bad" when you come off as an unimaginative and fairly dull.

Usage #3

The final way, and a more hit-or-miss way, to use better imagery is to use popular culture references to replace adjectives. The more widely known the reference is, the better the joke.

However, some people will completely miss the reference and not know what you're talking about. That's why this can be hit-or-miss.

This is very simple. Let's pick a well-known reference to use: the corruption of the Olympic Games. It's not something that people know details about, but it's something that people generally know exists. See – it's tough.

What traits would you assign to this reference? Corruption, unfairness, inequality, deviousness, sneakiness, and so on.

You can use the traits of the reference to describe things, such as "That cashier gave me a one dollar bill back instead of a ten dollar bill. Does he work for the Olympics or something?"

You're replacing the word "corrupt" with a popular culture reference – a much more descriptive, timely, and vivid way of speaking.

Let's use another well-known reference: the television show "Game of Thrones".

Use the traits of the television show to describe something – in this example, "addicting" – "This octopus pie is almost as addicting as watching 'Game of Thrones'. It's amazing."

The key is to get people to visualize the references and laugh from the disconnect.

With that said, make sure the references you use are appropriate. It pays to devote some attention to the ages and contexts of the people you're speaking to.

It only takes a little bit of effort to begin replacing the words and phrases in your vocabulary to sound like a completely new person. Unfortunately, we only get one chance to make first impressions on people, so make them count!

Chapter 9. The Art of Misconstruing

Some of the funniest situations I've seen in both movies and real life have come from simple misunderstandings.

Bob misunderstood what a proctologist did and scheduled four appointments, or Jenny misunderstood that the generic name for a painkiller is an analgesic, and is not pronounced nor administered the way she thought it was. Which one of those was from real life and which was from a movie? Well, both were from real life.

Those are instances of lightning caught in a bottle. Wouldn't it be great to create those moments when you want? You can take the lead instead of waiting for an opportunity to arise and essentially relying upon luck.

Misunderstanding and misinterpretation are great

sources of humor because you play with two sets of expectations and operating in the gray area between them.

Sometimes you have to be intentional about setting these misunderstandings yourself, and that is The Art of Misconstruing: misunderstanding people in an intentional manner to bring about a comical situation.

In other words, playing dumb or confused and taking an entirely different meaning from what someone has said on purpose. It's one of the easiest and quickest ways to bring the conversation to a playful nature and break the mold of small talk conversation.

Think of it as a transition from a boring topic into a more engaging conversation. Whatever perspective you take, it's simply a shift toward both parties enjoying themselves more.

The misconstruing tactic requires you to stay in character for a split second while you do it. Strangely and counter-intuitively, this requires people to think for a split second that you truly mean what you say. Otherwise, you convey mixed messages, and your words don't match up with the rest of your non-verbal or verbal delivery.

After that split second has passed, it will become obvious through your words and your delivery that you are obviously making a joke.

Here's a simplified example of misconstruing: when someone says "I like cats," you might reply with, "To EAT?" Pair your words with a shocked look on your face and eyes wide open. That's the character you are trying to convey.

You've misconstrued the other person by not picking up on their context or intent. Imagine how a foreigner might interpret those words because of a weak grasp of the English language. Where does the conversation go from there?

They'll likely join the banter with you and agree, such as "Yeah, but only stray cats. The domesticated ones are too fat."

Misconstruing is one of the most common ways of creating a humorous situation. It is the basis of many jokes because it's easy to take a situation and steer it in whatever direction you want. It allows you to initiate a joke with people in most situations.

It also helps you break out of typical, boring topics. By simply choosing to misconstrue, you can inject whatever perspective you want into a conversation at any point.

It's freeing and empowering! It doesn't get old and it can go a long way in adding life to otherwise a generic or boring conversations.

What are some ways to misconstrue in a funny way?

Exaggerated Conclusion

This is where you misconstrue what someone says and take it to the extreme conclusion.

You exaggerate what they say to an exponential degree. If someone actually said X, you would pretend that they said X multiplied by one hundred and react accordingly.

For example, when someone says "I love my television," you might reply, "So do your parents know that you guys are living together before marriage?"

Instead of saying "I agree", or coming up with a statement on the same vein, or at the same intensity with the original statement, take the original statement and blow it out of proportion and to a different context.

If somebody says a politician has a good point, a really funny exaggeration would be "Yes, he is the epitome of this country's political evolution, let's use him for breeding."

It is all about blowing up somebody's statement to an absurd and exaggerated form.

Another example: "That coffee was terrible!" you could reply, "I agree, my car's battery water is tastier."

What makes this form of misconstruing powerful is the absurdity of your exaggeration. It should be so absurd that it is no longer believable. That's where the humor comes from. A lot of people screw up this technique when they don't exaggerate enough.

They fall somewhere in between the truly funny exaggerated form and the generic statement. If you want to use this technique, make sure you really blow it up and make it out of this world. That way it's obvious to the other person that you are making fun and they can laugh along.

Playful Tease

This is when you misconstrue what they say to be negative about themselves.

Assume that they are making a self-deprecating statement and agree with them.

For example, when someone says, "I love watching television" you might say, "Yes, but you know that television doesn't replace friends, right?"

What did we do here? We assumed that they were lamenting the fact that they loved television and had no one to spend time with, so television was their only choice.

Misconstrue that they are being negative, and you are just agreeing with them.

If someone was to say, "I love this shirt," you might reply, "Don't worry, we'll go shopping for a shirt that *actually* looks good." You take the person's judgment and redirect it against them. With the right facial expressions, this statement will not come off as an attack. Instead, this will come off as a nice joke.

Finally, if someone was to say, "She's my favorite singer," you might reply, "We'll work on your taste."

Again, watch your facial expression. There is a thin line between teasing and downright insulting somebody. Make sure that all the other signals you send out from your body language, tone of voice, eye contact, and facial expressions convey the fact that you are just joking.

It goes without saying, but you need to be careful about this around sensitive people. Some people, no matter what you say, will take your words offensively and won't be able to take a playful rib. It's probably best to not use this tactic until you know people a little bit better, and definitely not about something you think they might be insecure about.

The other way of using the playful tease is to assume that *they* are insulting and being negative about you. Then you just react to that and act as if you are defending yourself.

Let's take the examples above, "She's my favorite

singer" and "I love this shirt." Misconstruing as if *they* are teasing *you* sounds like, "I know, my ears don't work because she's not my favorite," and, "So you're saying I could never pull that shirt off?"

If all else fails, you can just act shocked by the words and make a big deal out of them even though they said something fairly harmless. For example, when someone says "I love watching television," then you say, "Oh my gosh, television?!"

Another example is when someone says "That shirt is terrible," you say, "Terrible?! Are you crazy?!"

The bottom line is that misconstruing breaks people's expectations. It breaks the pattern of the conversation and spices it up. If done properly, you shake people out of the generic pattern of the conversation and highlight your sense of humor.

And as you can see, it's quite easy to jump in and out of conversation topics.

Chapter 10. The Power of Irony

Irony is a type of humor that is very close to sarcasm, and often confused with it.

Here's the official definition from Dictionary.com, just because it's something that people can struggle with nailing down: "the expression of one's meaning by using language that normally signifies the opposite, typically for humorous or emphatic effect."

Ironic humor is when something that is the exact opposite of what you might expect occurs. Another way to define irony is when you say something, but mean the exact opposite of what you expect.

In other words, the words that come from your mouth are the opposite of the emotion you are feeling. If you're starving, an ironic statement might be something like, "I'm so full I need to unbuckle my belt. It's like Thanksgiving in July."

Ironic humor draws its power from contrasts. There is a contrast between literal truth and perceived truth. In many cases, ironic humor stems from frustration or disappointment with our ideals. The things we imagine how the world should be produces comedy when it clashes with how the world actually is.

Ironic humor is usually used to make a funny point about something or to point something out. For example, when you see a bird landing on a sign that says "No birds allowed," that's ironic humor. The sign bans birds, but the bird is there sitting on the sign. The expectation that the sign ensures that there will be no birds in the vicinity failed.

Another example is when you see a car with a logo on the door saying "Municipal Traffic Reduction Committee," and the car, along with everybody else, is stuck in two hours of bumper to bumper traffic. There is a profound ironic comedy there as you would expect the traffic management planning committee would do a better job so they wouldn't be stuck in traffic themselves.

Irony is all about finding contrast and drawing some interesting and creative judgment out of it.

Ironic humor is when you intentionally imply the opposite meaning of what you say. When we think about how to use irony conversationally, what we're really thinking about is what ways can we convey two messages at one time?

Words Versus Tone

This is where you use your words to say one thing, but use your vocal tone to imply the opposite. You can use this when you express a stance, opinion, or feeling. You can say the following statements in a very funny, ironic way:

"I'M A PEOPLE PERSON! PEOPLE LIKE ME!" You would yell this in an angry and menacing tone.

"I am very happy right now. I am ecstatic. " This would be said in a very grumpy and exasperated voice.

"I'm going to kill you. You are so annoying." You would say this with a saccharine and overly-sweet tone.

You can go both ways on this: positive words with negative tone, or negative words with positive tone. You know you've done it correctly if it's apparent to the other person what you're trying to say. If you cause confusion when you try this method, it means that the tone of your voice isn't obvious enough.

Words Versus Body Language

This is where you use your words to say one thing, but your body language, facial expressions, and everything else non-verbal screams something different.

Imagine the same examples from the previous variation, but instead of your vocal tone, your body language and facial expressions are the opposite of your words.

"I'M A PEOPLE PERSON! PEOPLE LIKE ME!" would be said with a huge scowl, and making a knife motion across your neck to indicate that you hate people.

"I am very happy right now. I'm ecstatic," would be said while shaking your head, gesturing that you want to jump off a bridge, all with a disgusted face.

"I'm going to kill you. You're so annoying," would be said while smiling angelically, attempting to hug them gently, and stroking their shoulder gently as if to calm them down.

Ironic humor uses different elements that clash with each other to produce contrast in the mind of your audience. It creates a sense of the unexpected and excites the people you are speaking with. Its reason for being funny operates in a similar way to misconstruing. It is all about the contrast and creating an unexpected moment.

You can go both ways on this variation as well. You can pair positive words with negative non-verbal expression, or negative words with positive non-verbal expression. Of course, you can combine your non-verbals (body language and facial expressions), tone of voice, and actual words for greatest effect.

Ironic Simile

A simile is a literary device where you say one thing is like another thing. At least, that's a normal simile.

An *ironic simile* is a comparison between two things that are not similar at all, except for one shared trait or descriptor.

The way to use this for humor is to make a statement, and then compare it to something that is the exact opposite of what you are feeling. Explaining an ironic simile is like trying to explain what a color looks like, so here are a few examples.

"I'm as likely to vote for that candidate as I would set up an appointment with a narcoleptic proctologist."

You say that you would vote for the candidate, but then you introduce something that is supremely negative. That's ironic simile – a comparison to something that is the opposite of what you mean.

Most people wouldn't want to set up a exam with a narcoleptic proctologist. You wouldn't know when your physician would fall asleep and possibly leave something in an unfortunate place.

"I'm as sad as a dog with a bone."

Usually when a dog has bone on his mouth, the last emotion you would describe is sadness. Usually, dogs with bones are quite happy. When you say this statement, you mean the precise opposite.

"That person is as flexible as a brick."

The humor here is that you highlight the fact that this person is not flexible at all. Unless you are dealing with a brick made of super conducting jelly, chances are, the brick in question is extremely inflexible and rigid.

The process is, roughly, to first make a statement that is the opposite of how you actually feel, and then compare it to a situation that is also the opposite of how you feel.

Hyperbole

This is when you say something negative about a positive statement, or you say something positive about a negative statement – in a hyperbolic and exaggerated way.

"Flat tire? Best news of the week."

Negative occurrence, then positive statement.

Usually when people say something to this effect, they draw your attention to how negative or positive something actually was. Now that they got a flat tire, they have a new worry on top of the previous minor irritations and annoyances this week has delivered.

"It's not a problem, I'll probably run four miles later. It's only my ankle and foot!"

This is hilarious precisely because you are making light of the fact that you have a serious medical condition.

Irony is funny, but you shouldn't over use it, otherwise people won't know what you're saying, and people might not take you seriously at all. You're conveying a mixed message intentionally, so at some point people have to know your baseline personality and set of reactions.

Chapter 11. Instigate a Banter Chain

Have you ever noticed that some people seem to have witty, funny banter with everyone they meet?

It's not a coincidence. They are doing some of the exact things in this chapter to create that feeling whenever they want. It's easier than you think, but again, like most of the tactics here, you will be utilizing mental muscles that you haven't often used before.

There will be a slight learning curve, and you shouldn't expect to do it perfectly the first few times. That said, when you do grasp it more fully, you'll see the opportunities you've been missing to interact with people in certain ways. Also, the more you use it, the better you'll get at it.

One of the easy ways to inject humor in any kind of conversation is when you instigate and create a banter chain. A banter chain involves both parties and allows a playful exchange that feels collaborative.

What's a banter chain? Well, it sounds something like this...

A: "That's a heck of a pant suit you've got there."

B: "Thanks, I had trouble finding a skirt to fit over my powerful thighs."

C: "You're squatting about 250 pounds now, right?"

D: "Closer to 350 pounds. Dogs are afraid of me when I walk by."

E: "You could use them as a screen for a drive-in movie theater."

F: "Did that last week. The double feature paid my rent this month. Did you know the design for those two skyscrapers downtown was inspired by my legs?"

That's a banter chain. You can see how it was a flowing conversation and how both parties played off each other. It was a collaborative effort and sounded like something you might find in a television show. In fact, that's what most of us think of when we think about witty banter: we're going with the flow and creating conversational chemistry.

But, what just happened there and how can you do it? Let's take a step back for a second.

This is a unique type of humor. It's funny not based on what you say by itself, but how you play off the other person. If the other person catches on, then this gets funnier the farther along in the sequence that you get. The situation gets more absurd, but that's the part that is funny.

It quickly becomes apparent to everyone listening that something funny is happening, and they will want to contribute to the shared experience. A joke was initiated, and both people *stayed in the joke* for as long as they could.

When you say something and another person builds something on top of what you have said, you create an instant bond. This creates an instant comfort amongst everybody participating. It's as if somebody is passing around a bottle and sharing a story. It feels good to everybody because they feel that they are part of something, and this can produce very funny situations.

If you have been to a comedy improv club, the banter chain might seem familiar. It is essentially improv comedy, where you collaborate with the other person to build a scene, or conversation in this case. Improv comedy and conversation really have the same overall goal, so it's no surprise that the same techniques work for both.

If done properly, this chain of statements becomes

weirder, funnier, and more outrageous. Everyone involved takes ownership over this, and all come away feeling like you've worked on something together. At the very least, you're going to have a solid inside joke to build upon for further interactions.

Banter Chain Mechanics

Now we get back to the banter chain that started this chapter.

What happened there? A banter chain has a few main elements and a few rules. Once you learn the mechanics, you're off to the races and can see how you prefer to approach it.

First, you need to misconstrue something in some way to enter the banter chain.

That's what statement B (*Thanks, I had trouble finding a skirt to fit over my powerful thighs.*) was. It doesn't matter how you misconstrue it, all you're doing is moving off-topic. You can also make an assumption about the other person out of nowhere, exaggerate something about their characteristics, or even make a non-sequitur. What's important is that it's a non-serious statement that the other person is aware is a joke.

You've initiated a joke (not *made* a joke), and it's an invitation for them to join the banter on top of that joke.

Second, you have to see if the other person will play ball with you. When you make a non-serious statement, they'll either make a comment on it, or they will go back to the actual topic at hand. If they play ball, it looks like statement C (*You're squatting about 250 pounds now, right?*). If not, it would return to statement A (*That's a heck of a pant suit you've got there.*).

Third, if they play ball with you, congratulations! You're in a banter chain: they recognize what you're doing, they're playing along, and now you have to figure out how to play along back.

So, how do you do this? You build upon the direct response that they give you. You agree with them, and you add to it by *exaggerating and amplifying the sentiment*. That's what statement D (*Closer to 350 pounds. Dogs are afraid of me...*) does to statement C (*You're squatting about 250 pounds now, right?*), and so on. It takes the main sentiment of large thighs and makes the stakes bigger every time and plays with it in a creative manner.

The easiest way to continue the chain is to agree and amplify. You take what they say to be true, you agree, and then assume that the hyperbolic sentiment is true. If someone has big thighs, then to you, they have thighs that were the models for skyscrapers.

If they're still hanging with you, they'll do something

101

similar and *stay in the joke* – that's the key here. You're staying in the joke that you've initiated, and prompted them to do the same.

You can continue this ad nauseam until someone breaks, but at that point, you've probably built an hour's worth of rapport.

The banter chain can be very funny, but it depends on how it started and how it proceeds. Everyone involved makes the choice to either say "Haha, yeah," or actually participate in the banter chain.

Here is another example of a banter chain:

Normal statement: *"Hey, I like the coloring of that cat."*

Misconstrued statement to enter the banter chain: *"So, you think that cat is pretty sexy, huh?"*

Playing ball: *"Yeah, I want to ask it out on a date. You think I have a chance?"*

Hitting the ball back by agreeing and amplifying: *"Totally. Where will you take it? Something fancy?"*

More banter: *"Italian. Some wine, some cheese, maybe some place with seafood. Let's see where the night takes us. Cats are nocturnal, after all."*

The great thing about the banter chain is that it allows

you to make fun of each other and highlight a little bit of your wit and intelligence. It is not just about exaggerating what the previous person said, since anybody can do that. What makes you a good participant in a banter chain is when you make statement that is not only reasonable, but also funny because it is creative and also creates references.

Not only do you create a funny interaction, you are allowing each other to drop your guard. It creates a lighthearted moment. There is also a bond created because you are collaborating with each other.

As amazing as this humor approach can be, you need to practice a little in advance.

Don't try to do this by the seat of your pants the first time. As little bit of advanced preparation can go a long way. Practice exaggerating statements people say to you. How can you step it up in terms of absurdity and outlandishness? What are the extreme consequences of the people's statements? How many ways can you say that someone's thighs are huge without actually insulting them?

If someone said something, what is the silly, hyperbolic consequence of taking that beyond its logical conclusion?

It's also helpful to realize that much of the time you will be making fun of yourself and exaggerating negatives about yourself in ridiculous ways. You have to let go of your ego. You might be insulted by things people say, but remember that banter is supposed to be lighthearted and fun. Allow yourself to be the target and exaggerate negatives about yourself. If it makes you feel better, you're going to be insulting yourself in absurd ways that can't possibly be true or hit *too* close to home.

With proper practice and the right approach, a banter chain can make a conversation last a long time, simply by agreeing and amplifying.

Chapter 12. Skip the Middle Step

We've talked about a lot of *conversational* laugh tactics thus far, which means they are easier to create on the fly and in the midst of a conversation. Many of them are just funnier ways to reply to people, mindsets to adopt, or ways to instantly create light-hearted moments.

This chapter's tactic, skipping the middle step, can be used for that, but it's a bit closer to traditional joke structure. That means that it will take some practice to see how it really works for you since it takes more planning and setup.

As you can imagine, it's not easy to insert traditional jokes into a conversation. For the most part, it simply takes too much work to insert traditional jokes. You might be able to do this a couple times if you have entertaining stories in which you can control everything in your message, but conversation usually doesn't work that way, or have openings like that.

Normal conversations have their own flow, and traditional jokes almost always interrupt that flow. It can also interrupt the level of comfort both you and the person have established. The difficulty lies in the fact that a traditional joke has certain strict requirements. If it is missing something, it isn't going to fly. As we discussed earlier, if you miss just one element or vital piece of information, your entire joke or story falls apart.

Soon you may be able to use this chapter's tactic in normal conversation, but it might take longer than other tactics in this book.

The straightforward traditional joke structure that I'm speaking of is: (1) setup, (2) action, (3) punch line. It's very direct and simple, and observable below:

Setup: Knock, knock.
Action: Who's there? Lettuce. Lettuce who?
Punch line: Lettuce in, it's cold out here!

If the title of this chapter is "Skip the Middle Step", that means this laugh tactic is about skipping the middle action step, and going straight from the setup to the punch line. The above knock knock joke doesn't work with this method.

It sounds counterintuitive, but it works because of

what is implied. You only need to give the first and final part. Sometimes, it actually works better because you appear to be steps ahead of other people. Skipping the middle step allows you to insert a traditional joke into your conversation.

This approach can make you look like a professional comic as it would seem that you found a way to insert a formal and traditionally structured joke into your conversation.

As you can probably already tell, using this humorous approach is not second nature to most people. It isn't something that most people can just try on the fly and succeed. In fact, that statement probably applies to most of what's in this book, so don't feel bad if you don't find immediate success. There is absolutely a learning curve involved here.

There are four steps to using the laugh tactic of skipping the middle step. Of the four steps, the second step is silent and mental.

Step One

State a situation or scenario.

Step Two

State a funny conclusion or outcome of that scenario. This is the step that you skip out loud, but imply and allude to when you go straight from step one to step three.

Step Three

State a *cause* of that conclusion or outcome.

Step Four

Combine Step One and Step Three.

Here is an example of skipping the middle in action:

Step one: There is currently construction in my neighborhood.

Step two: Construction workers fall from ladders. This is the funny conclusion that you don't say out loud.

Step three: I was playing with marbles.

Step four (combining step one and three and skipping step two). What happens when you play with marbles around construction? People probably fall. Therefore: **There's a lot of construction in my neighborhood this week, fortunately I was playing with marbles, so it should end pretty quickly.**

It's tough to dissect and assemble four steps in the midst of a conversation, so this will require practice. The humor comes from the insinuation of the step that you skipped – the action – because it implies that you are causing that action. That's where the joke is.

There's a hint of mischief and the obvious interpretation is that you're willfully causing construction workers to fall so you can speed the construction along, although you haven't said that directly. You are implying the cause and step two.

It's much more clever and witty than simply saying, *"I am going to play with marbles, make the construction workers fall, and end construction early. Praise."*

Skipping the middle step allows others to connect the dots and come to the realization that you've done that and more already.

Here is another example of skipping the middle step in action:

Step one: I like to practice boxing.

Step two: I'm going to get my butt kicked at some point. (You'll be omitting this part.)

Step three: I'm going to get cocky and step into the ring with someone who thinks I'm as good as I talk.

Step four (combining step one and three): What happens when you step into the ring with someone who doesn't take it easy on you? *I love boxing, but sooner or later I'm going to step into the ring with someone who isn't paid to take it easy on me.*

One final example for clarity:

Step one: I love coffee.

Step two: I spilled the coffee all over my white shirt.

Step three: A dog ran in front of me.

Step four (combining step one and three): What happens when a dog runs in front of you when you are carrying an overflowing cup of coffee? *I love coffee, unless dogs run in front of me.*

Skipping the middle step requires a proper setup for it to work. It's easier to use than a traditional joke, but there has to be elements within the conversation that can be drawn for its structure. This is kind of an intermediate humorous approach.

What do you need to think about with skipping the middle step?

It is more difficult to use this technique spontaneously. However, if you have the time to think about a cause and effect, you can create what appears to be a professional joke.

Only after enough practice with other types of humor will this make sense because you know when to make the call. You learn know to insert this type of humor in the conversation. It will train you to think about what makes a setup and action humorous.

Chapter 13. The Six Questions Approach

This is another laugh tactic that takes some getting used to. It is more akin to a traditional joke structure.

However, once you get it down, you'll quickly see how to apply it in everyday life. You have to develop an eye and sense for it, but you'll find that developing those skills are beneficial to your conversations in general.

One of the main aspects of humor is surprise and playing with the unexpected. As we've explored in earlier chapters, it's funny to point out contrasts and defy expectations. It's funny if we imagine Arnold Schwarzenegger as a ballerina.

The six questions technique plays on this same vein of comedy, and it allows you to directly skip ahead to finding aspects of contrast and defied expectations.

We have certain expectations about every situation,

scenario, or story. To know what expectations we can play with and defy, it's important to know what the initial expectations are.

In other words, you can't play with the expectations unless you define them and are familiar with their baseline. You can't bend the rules in baseball if you don't know what they are to start with.

Context is vital to humor. To have the best chance of being funny, you have to know everything involved in the story, and that's what the six questions are for. You ask them, discover them, and then defy them.

The six questions are ones that you're familiar with:

1. Who is involved?
2. What is happening?
3. Why is it happening?
4. When is it happening?
5. Where is it happening?
6. How is it happening?

Every journalist knows these basic questions, and these are the key to creating laughter. But, that's only the first step. What do you do with these six questions to defy expectations and be funny?

The first step is to look at a scenario.

Second, you answer the six questions for that scenario in a normal, expected manner.

Third, for each question, write a contrary, silly, surprising, or outrageous answer.

Fourth, see how you can use these answers to create a funny scenario by changing one element to defy expectations. Simply combine and/or integrate them.

Let's take this process through an example.

Step one: *"I was walking to eat lunch outside."*

Step two (answering the six questions normally): Me, walking outside, because I was hungry, around 1:00 p.m., outside of my home, in my slippers.

Step three (answering the six questions in a contrary and surprising manner): Roller skating instead of walking, midnight instead of 1:00 p.m., because I was bored instead of being hungry, me and a cat instead of just me, walking to find a blood donor instead of to get lunch.

Step four (insert one of those different answers from step three into the overall situation): "I wish I had roller skated to lunch. It was so nice outside and my supervisors would have been surprised."

Introduce the different element into the scenario and see how it works. Justify its place in the sentence. It's not a "ha-ha" joke, but it's a way to inject humor and personality into your conversation. All you have to do is articulate what's happening, and change one or two of the elements involved.

Think of what would be inherently be funny about those changes and exaggerations. How can you make the situation unique and shocking? This is how you create an oddball situation. You create "what if" hypotheticals, you reveal how your inner train of thought works, you talk about your feelings and interests more openly, you provide more details than you would otherwise, and you gain a better sense of your every day contexts.

Break down the narrative based on those six questions and swap out the traditional and expected answers with something unique and unpredictable.

See if you can slice and dice the different answers to the six questions to come up with something outside the box, innovative, and creative, while remaining conversational. Knowing the details and boundaries of each scenario allows you to deviate from them. It's smart to have a general structure to work with.

Here's another example.

Step one: *"I'm waiting for you at a cafe."*

Step two (answering the six questions normally): Me, sitting inside, waiting for my friend, around 9:00 a.m., a short bus-ride away, in a suit because I have an interview later.

Step three (answering the six questions in a contrary and surprising manner): Me and a dog, anxiously pacing outside, wearing my lucky purple hoodie, at 9:00 p.m., a block away from my house, waiting for my friend to pick me up.

Step four (insert one of those different answers from step three into the overall situation): "I was waiting for you at that café, and luckily there was a random dog there to keep me occupied!"

All of us have quirks. By building on your quirks in a good way, you can create funny stories by swapping out the standard and routine answers to the six questions with something more unconventional.

There is a trick to this laugh tactic: it has to be believable, but it also has to be shocking and unusual enough. It's a fine line.

This is how you can tell a great comedian from a mediocre one. Great comedians are able to stay within the boundaries of probability while creating humorous situations. Mediocre comedians on the other hand are all too eager to just come up with something really weird and bizarre for its own sake and shock factor. When you do that, it doesn't work. It's obvious that you are trying too hard to be shocking. It is important to stay in the middle and try to come up with something probable and believable.

You can increase the impact of the six questions approach by injecting pop culture and topical references into step three.

For example, imagine if instead of roller skating out to lunch, you made a reference to a dance craze that was sweeping the nation, like the Macarena. Or, if instead of going out for lunch, you went out to get a type of tea that was just introduced into your country and every store is selling out of it.

These are the small details that make people feel involved, invested, and encourage them to listen to you more when you speak.

By introducing pop culture references, you can more thoroughly fill out the comedic dimensions of the description. You can alter the six questions with non-sequiturs, which do work, or you can alter them in ways that people can immediately relate to. Simply relying on the unexpected, the outlandish or the outrageous might not do the trick.

Don't become a victim of your own success when it comes to using exaggeration or unexpected answers to the six questions. One of the biggest killers of humor is overdoing it.

Proper pacing is important. You don't want to desensitize your audience, or annoy them at your lack of ability to give a real answer.

What I love most about the six questions approach is that it is a wonderful way to exercise your imagination and creativity. Humor doesn't stay in boxes. Boxes are for small talk with co-workers that we hate, and love to avoid.

Humorous conversations and being a better people person come from exercising thinking in non-linear ways, seeing alternate tracks of thought, connecting unrelated topics, and staying away from literal interpretations.

Remember that we want to change our entire goal orientation toward conversations and interactions. Whatever the case, you simply want to create an enjoyable interaction, and there are many ways to do that. In essence, that means your goal is to just play with people and get them to crack a smile. *Mess around with them*.

Let the alternate answers to these six questions be one of the ways that you enter that universe.

Chapter 14. Instant Role Play

One of the best ways to break out of interview mode is to engage in role play. Taking on a character, leaving yourself behind, and engaging in the ultimate type of *conversational play*.

Let's think about that from a bird's eye view.

You're stuck in an interview style of small talk conversation. There doesn't seem to be any hope of transitioning into a conversation that builds any meaningful rapport. You both feel too self-conscious and restrained in what you can talk about. You feel trapped, and to make things worse, the friend who gave you a ride won't be back for another hour or so.

Now, what if you decided to act like someone from a television show or movie? What if you actively imagined what that character would do in your situation and said it out loud?

Imagine that the other person went through the same exact process, and started playing the role of someone else. What would your conversation look like at that point?

Much better!

Therein lies the magic of role playing. Not only is it great for conversational play and amusement, it can break you out of conversational prisons. It allows you to say what you might not otherwise say, and act in ways that you normally would be too self-conscious to ever do.

It is playing around and injecting a lot of fun and informality into your conversation. You don't want to be stuck in a situation where you ask a question, the other person answers, then they ask a question, and you answer. In many cases, such exchanges are superficial and forgettable.

If you want to get the attention of the person and make a good impression, play around with them and do a little bit of role play.

Instant role play is easier to do than the tactics in the previous two chapters.

Skipping the middle step requires you to have timing and an eye for spotting opportunities. Similarly, asking six questions requires some practice in figuring out conversation patterns and coming up with variations.

Telling traditional jokes with its structural requirements requires the right topic and situation for it to make sense. That kills a lot of spontaneity and fun during a conversation. Until you get up to speed, it's usually a better decision to try more conversational laugh tactics, and instant role play is one of them.

Just like the scenario at the beginning of this chapter, role play takes you to a different mental arena where people use their wit and are aware that they work together with you during the conversation to keep playing out those roles.

You are creating an improvised comedy performance on the fly, and with this technique, you tell people what roles they will play so they will naturally comply with you. You are the one initiating the role play, and this allows people to follow you when they see a clear direction as to where to go with it.

At the root of it, role playing is fun. When you get into it, people will take off running. Whether or not we did choir or theater in school, it was fun to step into someone else's life, even for a short time.

At some point in our lives, we have tried to play a role, or we say ridiculous things that we normally don't say. We try to step into the shoes of somebody else and look at the world from their perspective and act accordingly. It engages many different aspects of our personal imagination and creativity. It's a great way to step out of our daily routine and roles.

Most people welcome role playing because our personal roles can get restrictive in reality. For example, your role is a son, a friend, a boyfriend, an employee, and so on and so forth. It is too easy to define yourself based on your roles instead of who you really are.

Most people jump at the opportunity of breaking out of their daily lives with role playing. Think about how empowered you feel when you wear a mask during Halloween and become anonymous.

So, what are the steps in role playing?

Step one: make a "judgment" statement about someone.

The trick is that the statement has to put them in contrast to you. It has to make them relatively better, worse, funnier, happier, crazier, or calmer than you. It can be a compliment, or a playful tease, as long as you can contrast yourself to them with it.

For example, you can give them a compliment. This puts them in a superior role to you. You might say, "Your sense of style is so amazing, I wish I had it too." This statement implies that the other person has better taste in clothing than you. Relative to you, they are superior in this regard.

A tease, on the other hand, puts them in an inferior role to you. For example, when you say "Nice jacket. Do they make it for women?" the implication is that they can't tell the difference between and men's and women's jackets, and they need help dressing themselves. Relatively speaking, you are superior to them in this regard.

You aren't judging them, but you are making a statement that assigns a value to them in this regard.

Step two: give them a label based on the statement that you made.

Here you'll see the reason it is so important that the statement you made in step one assigns a relative value to them.

For example, if you give somebody the compliment "Wow, you are great at navigating," continue on and give them a title or label, such as "Milwaukee's very own Magellan," or "my go-to personal GPS during road trips."

If you went the opposite way and teased someone with "you are terrible at navigating," you would give them a title or label such as "You are like Lewis and Clark but blind" or "Google Maps but offline."

It is important that you actually give them a title or label, versus just describing how good or bad they are relative to you. It's important because... **that's the role they will be playing**!

Step three: starting playing the roles!

Whatever title or label you have given them, that's the other person's role.

What is your role? This is why the role needs to be relative to you: you can either be someone who is learning from that person, or someone who is teaching that person.

For example, if someone is the *modern day Magellan*, then that's their role, and your role is to be curious about how they learned their craft and got so good at it. If you elevate someone, then your role is inferior to them.

If someone is *Google Maps but offline*, then their role is inferior to you, and you take the role of teaching them. If you playfully tease someone down, your role is superior to them.

Spell out the roles, and then act in them. This is crucial to the humor. You have to remain consistent.

This is how it sounds all put together from top to bottom:

"You are so great with maps and navigating, I can't believe it. You're like a modern day Magellan."

"Oh, thanks, man. I've just done it a lot."

"No, you're Magellan. Which continent did you most enjoy discovering?" (This is where you've assigned them their role, and are literally putting them into it and asking them to embrace it.)

"Oh... probably South America. The fruit is so good there." (Here, they catch on that you are role playing. Not everyone will catch on immediately, or at all. If they catch on, they will stay in character and continue with the tone you've set.)

"Yeah, that makes sense. Did you interact with the locals?"

"All the time!"

"Did you men enjoy the locals or the fruit more?"

"Hard to say..."

So, what happened there? I explicitly told them their role, and it came from the title that I gave them because of a compliment. The compliment was hyperbolic and exaggerated as those are the easier types of roles and characters to play.

It's much easier to play someone who is incredibly insane versus mildly disturbed, right?

After the person realizes what is happening, it's up to you to keep the role play going. You've created the roles, the situation, and you have to continue to guide it.

You might also have noticed that once you're into the role play, it seems similar to a banter chain as we discussed in an earlier chapter. To continue to guide the role play, just take their statement, stay in character, agree, and amplify it.

As you can see, instant role play is easier to instigate than you think. It allows you to blow through conversational impasses and enter a mode of thought where you are playing with the other person. It's a much better mindset for rapport, and more conducive to making friends than beginning with small talk and trying to transition from there.

Chapter 15. The Comic Triple

The comic triple is one of the easiest and most recognizable jokes in the world.

You may not realize it, but you've heard this many, many times in your life. It's about time to learn how to use it effectively!

Before we dive into the mechanics and steps, here's a quick example of the comic triple.

You know what my favorite part about coffee is? The energy boost, the aroma, and the yellowing effect on your teeth.

The comic triple draws its power from the fact that people have been conditioned in many ways to process information and take significance in groups of threes.

Think about where this pattern of threes exists in our lives. It's everywhere.

The Three Little Pigs. Newton's three laws of physics. *Goldilocks and the Three Bears.* The three parts of a joke. The three phases of a story. Destiny's Child. *Charlie's Angels.* Kirk, Spock and Dr. McCoy. The Three Stooges. The Holy Trinity.

There is something about the number three and how the brain organizes itself.

Once you start looking, you'll see it everywhere. For good reason, it's also the method management experts use to most effectively teach and disseminate information. For example, notable leadership expert Kevin Kruse is known for only giving people three pieces of information at a time. This way, people can maintain their focus and not get distracted. Some argue that if you can't boil something down to three main points, it's not an inherently sound argument.

You can even put it this way: the human brain is certainly capable of retaining more, but for greatest impact, comedic or not, three works best.

That is the background for why the triple is indeed the comic *triple*.

When you make a list of three things, you generally make a list of three similar things. They might even be synonyms. For example, you might describe a woman as sexy, cute, and beautiful, or a new type of car as exciting, cool, and innovative.

When you make any type of list, you build an expectation that you'll be enhancing the sentiment, and using the list to emphasize one point overall. People expect only one direct line of thinking.

The comic triple surprises people because where they might expect a list to contain only one sentiment, the comic triple contains two, and the two sentiments couldn't be more different.

The first two elements are something expected and in line with each other. They are relevant to each other and flow naturally from each other, the third is what springs the surprise on the hearer. The tension of the buildup is released, and the surprise makes people laugh. Again, what makes this work is the surprising and unexpected nature of the third element.

Let's bring this out of the abstract and into the concrete for a moment: the first two elements will be positive, and the last element will be negative, or vice versa. Now we can continue with less confusion.

One famous example of the comic triple is from Mark Twain, made in reference to government data and how to analyze it: "There are lies, damned lies, and statistics."

Everyone hates being lied to. We are outraged when

people in government, or those taking advantage of the government's influence, lie to benefit themselves. We're so outraged that we go along with the "damned lies" part because it's more of the same insidious manipulation of the public. We're enraged. We expect the last part of this list to build to the epiphany of corruption with something like, "the lies that make you unable to sleep at night."

That's the logical conclusion, right?

Instead, we're thrown for a complete loop when Twain mentions statistics. Statistics are the opposite of lying, assuming they are not being manipulated or faked. People instinctively trust statistics. Therefore, this is the exact opposite sentiment of the first two elements of Twain's triple.

Here's another example of a comic triple from comedian Chris Rock: "There are only three things women need in life: food, water, and compliments."

That quote is funny because food and water go together. The sentiment is simply based on sustenance and basic human needs. Usually, when people say you only need three things to survive, the third element people are probably anticipating is air or shelter.

Chris Rock dashes your sense of anticipation and expectation by completing the triple with "compliments," which is a small jab at women, as well as the opposite sentiment of a basic human need.

Here is another example from comedian Jon Stewart, former host of *The Daily Show*: "I celebrated Thanksgiving in an old fashioned way. I invited everyone in the neighborhood to my house, we had an enormous feast, and then I killed them and took their land."

Two positives and one negative. Are we seeing the pattern yet?

Jon Stewart is making fun of the history of Native Americans and European settlers in the United States. When the first English settlers came to New England they had such a tough time that they almost starved to death. It is only when a Native American showed them how to pick the right berries, prepare the right food, and otherwise survive in that new environment that they were able to raise enough food and the colony survived.

To commemorate that, the United States has celebrated Thanksgiving in some form or another since 1863. Stewart pokes fun at that traditional Thanksgiving in the historical context and also reminds people of the violence that went with the colonization of the United States. Two positives and one negative.

How do you make the comic triple work for you?

Step one: think of your topic or theme.

For example, we'll use the theme of coffee.

Step two: list two positives, or list two negatives.

List two things that are related to coffee in positive or negative ways.

For example, being energetic, waking up, having a routine, the aroma; these are generally positive descriptors that you might think about when you think of coffee.

Step three: list one negative, or one positive.

You go the opposite route, the opposite sentiment as what you used in step two.

So what's negative about coffee? This sets up the contrast. Stained teeth, being over-caffeinated, drug cartels, addiction, and spilling it on white clothing.

Step four: put it all together.

"I have coffee every morning. I love the aroma, how it wakes me up, and how I always seem to spill it on my white shirts."

Do you see how the anticipation and expectation builds through the first two elements, and then is completely reversed in the last element?

Here's another example now that we've gone through the process once. This time, we'll deconstruct a completed comic triple: "I love everything about her. Her smile, her sense of style, and how she never has any clue where she wants to go for dinner."

You take a person, and start with two positives, then you reverse the emotion and go negative.

Don't expect to hit a home run the first time you step up to the plate with this comedic approach. It can be mastered after a bit of practice. Keep it simple, and try to think in black and white and negative and positive terms.

Once you get good at the comic triple, you'll be able to assemble it on the fly. That's one of the best parts – you can list two positive aspects while brainstorming for the third, negative aspect, all spontaneously.

Chapter 16. Sarcasm? No way.

Sarcasm is a way for people to say things without saying them.

Think about how Chandler Bing from the television show *Friends* talks. If he says something is wonderful, he says *it's wonnnnderful* in a tone that immediately lets you know that he thinks the opposite.

Sarcasm functions like a social cue – both are ways to express something without having to explicitly say it.

In that way, it's a great device for handling uncomfortable topics or pointing out the elephant in the room without directly offending people (or pointing). It allows us to walk a tightrope, as long as we don't fall into the pit of passive-aggressiveness.

At some level, most of us can appreciate sarcasm because we know what is being accomplished. It can even be the basis for your own personal brand of humor. Standup comics often use it to great effect.

Chances are, you are already using it regularly without being fully aware of it.

This chapter is about arming you with the exact elements of most sarcasm that you can use expertly for better conversations, banter, and humor.

Sarcasm is mostly used as friendly banter with a friend or acquaintance with whom you are comfortable saying something negative.

Sarcasm is usually used to poke fun at someone or something, and is heavily context and audience dependent. If you are around somebody who enjoys wit and has a sarcastic sense of humor, it will be quite welcome.

But around others who don't share the same sense of humor, are less secure, or don't like you, it's too easy for them to interpret your attempts at sarcastic humor as a full-fledged insult. They might just think that you are an insulting jackass. That's not what you're aiming for here.

Using it in the wrong context will cause people to think you lack empathy or, worse, get your jollies from hurting other people's feelings.

However, choose the correct context and sarcasm can make you more likeable and charming. It also makes you look intelligent and witty. In some social circles, appropriate levels of sarcasm are not only welcomed, but required.

Now that you have a clearer idea about the proper context of sarcasm, the next step is to articulate the elements to make sure you don't just insult people left and right in your attempts at building rapport. If your annoying coworker understood sarcasm better, they might be as funny as they think they are.

For the most part, **sarcasm is saying the *opposite* of (1) an objective fact, (2) a subjective emotion, or (3) thought.**

It makes a contradictory statement about a situation to either emphasize or downplay its effect.

Objective fact: Bob plays Tetris at work constantly.

Sarcastic statement: *Bob, you are the busiest man I know.*

Subjective emotion or thought: It is hilarious that Bob plays Tetris at work constantly.

Sarcastic statement: *Bob deserves a medal for worker of the year.*

Here's another one.

Objective fact: There is a surprising amount of traffic lately.

Sarcastic statement: *What are we going to do when we get to our destination super early?*

Subjective emotion or thought: I hate traffic so much.

Sarcastic statement: *This traffic is the best part of my day.*

That's the first and most common use of sarcasm. Let's lay out a framework for different types of sarcasm and exactly when and how you can use it. You'll be surprised how formulaic and methodical you can get with this, and subsequently with humor.

When someone says something or does something very obvious, you respond by saying something equally obvious.

Bob: "That road is very long"

You: "You are very observant."

Bob: "It's so hot today!"

You: "I see you're a meteorologist in training."

Poor Bob: "This menu is huge!"

You: "Glad to see you've learned to read!"

The next application of sarcasm is when something bad happens. You say something about how that good or bad event reflects on the other person.

If it's good, you say that it reflects badly on them; if it's bad, you say it reflects well on them.

Bob: "I dropped my coffee mug."

You: "You've always been so graceful."

Bob: "I got an F on my math test."

You: "Now I know who to call when my calculator breaks."

You observe Poor Bob dropping a cup of coffee and state "You would make a great baseball catcher. Great hands!"

Proper delivery is crucial for sarcasm. This can mean the difference between people laughing at your sarcastic joke, or thinking that you're serious in your sentiment and an overall jerk.

You have to make it clear that you're being sarcastic and give them a sign indicating so. Otherwise, people will feel uncomfortable at the uncertainty. Are you just being mean, or are you trying to be funny?

The most common way to do this is with a combination of a deadpan vocal tone and a wry smile or smirk. With deadpan delivery, you don't laugh while you're saying it; you appear completely serious. Then, you break into a smile to alleviate the tension and clue them into your true intention.

Now that you know when to deliver sarcastic remarks, it's also important to learn about how to receive them and be a good audience. Let's pretend that you are Poor Bob from earlier, and insert a reply for him.

Bob: "That road is very long"

You: "You are very observant."

Bob: "You know it. I'm like an eagle."

Bob: "It's so hot today!"

You: "I see you're a meteorologist in training."

Bob: "I can feel it in my bones. It's my destiny."

Poor Bob: "This menu is huge!"

You: "Glad to see you've learned to read!"

Redeemed Bob: **"I can also count to ten."**

You need to amplify their statement and what they are implying. Does this look familiar? It's a self-deprecating remark + a witty comeback!

When you respond to sarcasm this way, it creates a greater bond. Everybody is comfortable, and you create a funny situation and potential for greater banter.

And just as important, you don't come off as a bad sport or someone who can't take a joke.

A lot of people who rely on sarcastic humor, pretty much on an automatic basis, are actually masking passive-aggressive personalities. They're constantly using sarcasm as a defense mechanism to hide their true feelings. They use sarcasm to pass off their otherwise negative emotions. They might be doing this to you, so it's important to know how to sidestep their subconsciously vicious attacks.

Sarcasm? It's *soooooo lame,* isn't it?

Chapter 17. The Witty Comeback Machine

As a former fat kid, I used to have a fairly extensive library of witty comebacks for those charming people who liked to point out that I was, indeed, still as fat as I was the day before.

Or that they couldn't ride in a car with me for fear of it tipping over.

Or that I was so big my Polo brand sport shirt had a *real* horse on it (this one was pretty clever, I'll admit).

Mind you, I wasn't really that large – just 20 pounds overweight. At some point, however, I developed one type of comeback that never failed to either shut people up, or bring them to my side through laughter.

Were you also aware that my Polo Sport shirt can be used as a parachute?

You better put six extra wheels on your car for me!

What exactly are these lines composed of, and why are they so effective?

Becoming a witty comeback machine is easier than you think, and it's one of the best conversational tactics you can learn. It doesn't only rear its head when dealing with insults – it is widely applicable once you learn the framework. If it's a bad situation, a witty comeback can diffuse the tension and bring emotional levels back to normal. If it's a good situation, then a witty comeback can make it even better.

Whatever the situation, mastering witty comebacks will earn you the respect of other people for your clever wit. It just takes one line – and the shorter and punchier, the better and more effective.

A witty comeback does many things simultaneously. It makes people laugh and disarms them, while allowing you to appear smart, insightful, and mentally quick.

Before I get ahead of myself, let me define what a witty comeback is.

Wit is essentially spontaneous creativity. You take a topic or statement and see it from a different angle in a way that is relatable, yet novel. That's why I kind of enjoyed the aforementioned joke about the Polo Sport shirt, even if it was at my expense.

Witty comebacks can be hurtful, serious, or

completely light and harmless. It all depends on you. You can be joking and playing around, or you can wield a sharp sword.

For the purposes of this book, you want to use wit to disarm people. So it's the former you should aim for, lest you create major tension. There's a fine line between destructive and teasing.

What's tricky about wit is that something that may be funny and completely harmless to you can be destructive or hurtful to someone else. You have to know where that fine line is and you have to know how to straddle it.

There are a few tricks to always having a witty comeback in your pocket ready for launch instead of 20 minutes after the encounter.

First, when thinking about a witty comeback, don't think generically.

Don't use, "I know you are, but what am I?" or "So is your mom." A witty comeback is judged by people based on how original it is – remember, it's spontaneous creativity. Using something that is both generic and unclever is decidedly neither spontaneous nor creative. Don't just use a generic or template-driven witty comeback that you've seen in a movie or something that better works in a totally unrelated context. And don't use one of the comebacks you thought were hilarious when you were ten. Those don't work anymore.

Second, don't act like you can't take a joke.

Of course, witty comebacks need an initial statement to "comeback" to.

The vast majority of the time, people are indeed joking when they say something negative about you in your presence. In a sense, it's a compliment because they assume you have a sufficient sense of humor and the emotional resiliency to deal with it. The people who *aren't* involved in jokes and good natured ribbing don't have many friends.

If you let it show that you are angry or hurt, it spoils the playful tone you could otherwise enhance with your witty comeback.

For example, if someone made a joke about my fatness, and I got visibly angry, they would likely stop... then walk on eggshells around me for days. When someone is uncomfortable with something, they make others uncomfortable as well. If that happens enough times, then it becomes clear that I don't have a sense of humor and I let my insecurity infect my relationships.

Handle the initial negative statement with a wry smirk and with the knowledge that you are about to crush them.

Third, use the right tone.

The best witty comebacks are delivered with 50% indifference. When you deliver one with 100% excitement and 0% indifference, guess what happens? You blow it and the comeback falls flat. Indifference is the correct tone because comebacks are about your attitude – pretend that you are James Bond delivering a witty retort after a failed murder attempt by a villain. 50% indifference also ensures that you aren't being aggressive or hateful.

A witty comeback is the verbal equivalent of judo or aikido – using an opponent's words against them. If you take that analogy, you need a certain amount of cool to effectively counteract. Witty comebacks take the power away from the insult hurled.

There are four main types of witty comebacks.

None are better than the other. You just need to pick the type you're most comfortable with.

Type #1: Pick apart their words.

Think about the other person's word choice and quickly analyze whether there is another angle or meaning to those words. An easy approach is to interpret their words as overly literal or outlandish. The key is to interpret them in a way that is favorable to you to make it seem as if they complimented you instead of put you down.

Bob: *You are working as slow as a glacier. Pick it up!*

You: [focusing on the word glacier] *You mean I'm super strong and cool under pressure? True.*

Type #2: Agree and amplify.

The idea here is to agree with whatever the insult was, and then add to it in an absurd way. You amplify the initial sentiment to a degree that is ridiculous. This was my go-to technique to deflect jokes about my weight.

If you forgot from earlier in this chapter:

Were you also aware that my Polo Sport shirt can be used as a parachute?

You better put six extra wheels on your car for me!

For another example:

Bob: *Your cooking was pretty terrible last time.*

You: *You're lucky you didn't stay until the end of the night, we all got our stomachs pumped. Dinner at my place later tonight?*

Type #3: Reverse and amplify.

This is a simple deflection. This is when you get back

at them in a subtle way. When someone says you are bad at X, you basically turn it around by saying that they are even worse at X.

It's the exact same as the previous type of witty comeback, except instead of directing the amplification at yourself, you direct it to the other person.

Bob: *Your cooking was pretty terrible last time.*

You: *Yeah, but at least I didn't need to get my stomach pumped the way I did after you cooked last time!*

Type #4: Use an outlandish comparison.

This brings the conversation into a different sphere and makes both people laugh at the weird outlandish imagery. What makes this work is that the comparison, although extreme, is still somewhat realistic. To use the same framework, you're amplifying (to yourself or the other person) with an analogy here.

Bob: *Your cooking was pretty terrible last time.*

You: *True, I should have used the eggs as hockey pucks, right?*

Witty comebacks are the blood of witty banter, which is being able to take an element of what was said and attack it from a different angle without missing a beat.

You should be able to see how this can play out. They are instant retorts that aren't hostile or combative, while addressing something gracefully. What more can you ask for?

Word of caution: fight the temptation to rattle them off one after the other. Again, you have to remember that your goal is to get people to like you. You're not trying to prove a point or protect your pride.

You're just trying to keep your conversation from hitting awkward spots and dying a premature death. Firing off one comeback after another can kill whatever level of comfort you've managed to create because you will appear insecure, defensive, and full of bluster.

Wit comes naturally. There's an effortless quality to it.

Chapter 18. Five Quick Comic Quips

This chapter contains some of the best ways to get laughs, but I only wanted to cover them more briefly because they are relatively simple – hence the chapter title, quick comic quips.

These are little phrases, ways of thinking, and comedy techniques that can take you a long way if you use them right.

Schadenfreude

The best way to explain the concept of schadenfreude is with the story of two hunters.

There were two hunters out in the woods and they came across a huge bear. The bear turned and looked at them. It looked like it was getting ready to pounce at the hunters. One of the hunters then quickly knelt down and started putting on his running shoes. The other hunter looked in shock at the first hunter and said, "What are you doing? Do you think you are going to outrun this bear? It's impossible, this bear is going to lunge at us and kill both of us. You can't run that fast!"

The first hunter said "Well, I only need to run faster than you."

Schadenfreude is the pleasure you receive when something bad happens to somebody else.

While schadenfreude is a German term, it applies universally to all cultures. A lot of us have experienced this guilty sense of pleasure when we hear or observe that something bad has happened to somebody we know. In fact, I suspect part of the reason social media is popular is people looking for their daily fix of schadenfreude.

For example, a Facebook "buddy" might have made it his personal mission to post pictures of himself traveling all over the world. You scroll through his updates showing off riding elephants in Thailand, pushing back against the Leaning Tower of Pisa, or borrowing an oar off a (annoyed) gondola pilot in Venice.

His most recent update is definitely more downbeat. He just got through a harrowing experience trying to get from Thailand to Myanmar and was detained by Burmese border guards for over a week until the

154

proper "processing fee" changed hands.

It's funny because someone else is in worse shape than you, even momentarily, and however you view yourself is boosted. Your buddy's life seems perfect, but at least you haven't been detained by border guards.

Or what about when your neighbor's spoiled teenage son, who has always annoyed you and gotten away with his mischief, breaks a finger after falling from his shiny new bike? Classic schadenfreude.

In a sense, schadenfreude reflects the fact that misery loves company. Life is full of ups and downs, and one way we can comfort ourselves is when we feel a sense of pleasure when something worse happens to somebody else.

We don't *want* bad things to happen to other people, but we do feel a relief of tension when we realize that "Wow, it's not just me" and "Well, things could be worse!"

Schadenfreude works because there is a tension that is built and released when we observe people in slight suffering. Laughing eases that tension and smoothes it over.

To intentionally use it to get a laugh, you can either point out small failures and misfortunes of you or your conversation partner.

It's best to not dwell on other people's shortcomings. That's criticism, and a very fine line to walk. You should focus on yourself and emphasize your own misfortunes. Appeal to other people's sense of schadenfreude with self-deprecating humor.

Acknowledge the Elephant in the Room

A quick comic quip is to acknowledge the elephant in the room, which is something people actively try to avoid mentioning or giving attention to.

Sometimes it's an uncomfortable truth that people tip-toe around, and sometimes it's something relatively simple, like the fact that someone's new haircut is terrible.

There are always inconvenient truths that most people know and are aware of, but are walking on eggshells to avoid.

When you acknowledge the elephant in the room, you end up releasing a lot of comedic tension, even with the person who might be the butt of the joke.

Why? Because you say out loud what everybody is already thinking.

Everybody knows there is a problem, or there is something weird, or there is something off, but they are just too polite to say it or they just don't go around to saying it for some reason. The best way to acknowledge elephant in the room is to do it in a sarcastic tone. This is what releases the tension.

For example, if you have a meeting in a sweltering room, you say something like "Thanks for coming everyone, let me know if you want some hot chocolate to warm up, I know it's cold in here."

If you are waiting to order at a bar and the bartender is taking a long time, you can say to your friend something like "I'm so glad the service here is so fast. It'll keep me from getting too drunk tonight!

Finally, "It's a good thing it's raining so hard, I haven't bathed in weeks!"

Acknowledging the elephant in the room is all about pointing out the obvious, but not in a judgmental or harsh way.

Stating What You See

Stating what you see is what it sounds like: Stating what you see in literal terms.

You point things out in their most literal and descriptive form. You are simply observing and calling out what you see with your own eyes.

Surprisingly, it takes practice to be able to ignore a contextual definition and actually say what you see. It was much easier when we were children and didn't understand more abstract terms and concepts. We thought about things in literal and descriptive terms.

And that's another way to look at it: think in terms of how a child might describe an observation, and be creative and vivid with it.

One of my favorite examples of this is to character a female's derriere as "two Pringles hugging."

A building might look like a dwarf wearing a Mexican sombrero.

A cloud might look like a spitting bear.

A car may be shaped like a melted bathtub. And so on.

You're making an observation and breaking it down into basic elements of shape, color, size, weight, and dimensions. It's creative, unique, and can be funny if you approach things in ways that no one has thought about. It might be a stretch that the car is shaped like a melted bathtub, but you're introducing a moment into people's lives where they think abstractly and are led down your line of thinking.

Misdirection

Misdirection is when you say one thing and then proceed with an immediate opposite.

For example, "It's a secret, but let me tell you immediately," or, "That show is great, except for everyone in it."

It seems confusing, but what you are doing is breaking a sentence into two parts.

You're stating something in the first part, then contradicting it immediately in the second. People won't immediately be sure of what you mean, and part of the humor comes from this introduced confusion. You have both positive and negative, or vice versa, in the same sentence.

The second part of the sentence is the part that people will react to, while the first part is typically the setup. The second part is your true sentiment on the topic.

Here's another example, "I love dogs, but I hate seeing, hearing, and touching them," or, "This juice is awesome. Did it come from the garbage disposal?"

Why does misdirection work?

Most of us try to be polite to people. We use euphemisms frequently, and we don't say what we really feel. The first part of a misdirecting statement is what people expect— politeness. Then, you contradict yourself and give them a dose of reality, which sets up a humorous contrast since you have deviated from what most people expect and would say themselves.

Last but not least, misdirection is a funny way to express your feelings on something. If you really feel X about a topic, then use misdirection! "Opposite of X, but actually X," will almost always be received far better than "Gosh, I hate X."

Reactionary Humor

Sometimes if you want to be funny, all you need to do is react.

You don't have to proactively say or do anything. It's the way you react to something mundane or funny that makes *you* funny.

This is called, predictably, *reactionary humor*.

In many cases, this is a more reliable form of being funny because you don't need anything, and you can rely on other people to play off of.

All we need to do to be funny is to simply react to the situation in front of us by tapping your inner reservoir of extreme reactions. That's the key here. For any comedic effect to happen, it has to be an extreme and exaggerated reaction, otherwise there's too much ambiguity about what you actually think.

For example, if we see a homeless woman dancing to loud Michael Jackson music, you might look over slack-jawed to your friend with an astonished face and wide eyes. Take your normal reaction of confusion and shock to the extreme, and that's what you should be showing.

That's an exaggerated reaction that can be funny because your reaction says, "What the heck is going on?" You're drawing attention to the big contrast between what you see and what is a more normal situation.

It's not that the homeless woman dancing to Michael Jackson is inherently funny, it's your reaction.

Reactionary humor doesn't require a language, or certain information. All you need is something to react to that people can see in plain sight, and then you can convey an exaggerated emotion to draw attention to the absurd.

You contrast the situation you're in and your evaluation of it. As with the above example with the homeless woman dancing, the emotion you showcase is confusion and shock: that is the first and easiest way to react in a funny way.

One good example of this is the character Jim in the British version of the television series "The Office." Jim's boss, Michael Scott, is ridiculous and outlandish, but recognizable. Jim isn't inherently funny, but what makes him funny is the way he reacts in shock and disbelief when he's faced with Michael's absurdities.

In many scenes from "The Office," Jim simply looks at the camera as if shocked, and the audience back home laughs. He set up the contrast between his inner monologue and the situation at hand.

This also works, because when we see his reaction, we know it's exactly the reaction that we would have, too. It puts a face to our inner thoughts and is like exchanging a knowing glance.

Reactionary humor is all about exploring the tension between what is perceived to be normal versus the zany and outlandish. The perceived normal is just what a normal person might think of a particular situation, and zany and outlandish is an abstract interpretation of what's actually occurring.

When you find yourself reacting as a straight-laced, normal person to an otherwise bizarre situation, realize that this is an opportunity for humor.

For the rest of us, you have to know the elements involved.

You have to understand that you're essentially playing the "straight man." It's a comedy term meaning that you are the foil around which crazy characters can interact with. Next, you allow the crazy characters to be crazy because there has to be someone to counterbalance the insanity.

To make this work for you, you have to be honest and ask yourself what role you usually play in life. Are you the straight and sane person normally giving the commentary, or are you the crazy and zany person who goes through all that funny stuff?

Reactionary humor is all about pointing out how crazy you think something is. It puts other people into your shoes and creates understanding about the situation. You have to pair this with a deadpan delivery to either someone's joke or to a weird situation.

Conclusion

There's a lot of information in this book. It may seem overwhelming and like you will never master it.

There's a reason there are only a few comedians you can name off the top of your head, and even fewer that are universally loved. It's *tough business* to be funny on command.

But there are only so many patterns, templates, and rules that people use – they are just used in creative ways that become possible after practice and exposure.

I know I won't be quitting my day job to become a standup comedian anytime soon, but there's no question about it – these laugh tactics make me exponentially funnier on a daily, conversational basis, and enable me to think quickly on my feet through a *funny* mindset.

And you know what? That is probably your goal as well – to become a bit more charming and witty with your friends and the opposite sex. Stay focused and go tactic by tactic. Practice and apply until it becomes habitual – then you can play with the rules themselves!

Until then, think fast!

Sincerely,

Patrick King
Social Interaction Specialist
www.PatrickKingConsulting.com

P.S. If you enjoyed this book, please don't be shy and drop me a line, leave a review, or both! I love reading feedback, and reviews are the lifeblood of Kindle books, so they are always welcome and greatly appreciated. I've worked really hard to present some value for you, and I always want to hear if I achieved that goal.

Other books by Patrick King include:

Conversation Tactics: Strategies to Command Social Situations: Wittiness, Banter, Likability

Speaking and Coaching

Imagine going far beyond the contents of this book and dramatically improving the way you build relationships and interact with the world.

Are you interested in contacting Patrick for:

- A social skills workshop for your workplace
- Speaking engagements on the power of conversation and charisma
- Personalized social skills and conversation coaching

Patrick speaks around the world to help people improve their lives through the power of building relationships with improved social skills. He is a recognized industry expert, bestselling author, and speaker.

To invite Patrick to speak at your next event or to inquire about coaching, get in touch directly through his website's contact form at http://www.PatrickKingConsulting.com/contact, or contact him directly at Patrick@patrickkingconsulting.com.

Cheat Sheet

Chapter 1. The Real Power of Being Funny

Humor is one of the most positives forces in life, and you can use that positive force to overcome obstacles, gain perspective, provide comfort, and create happiness in times of negativity and pessimism.

Chapter 2. The Unbreakable Rules of Comedic Delivery

Your delivery and manner of presenting a story or joke has ten times the comedic effect as your actual words. Know the primary emotion you want to create, know your primary goal, and above all else, never laugh first.

Chapter 3. Creating a Mindset for Humor

The mindset for being funny is simple – what would a five-year old do? You are acting as a professional adult far too often and need to embracing playing, misconstruing in a playful manner, and thinking non-linearly far more than discussing and conversing.

Chapter 4. Common Mistakes in Jokes and Humor

Common mistakes and bad habits for humor include being far too generic and relying on cheap laughs, rushing to or through your punch lines, leaving vital information out, and not being able to read how people are genuinely reacting through their fake or real smiles.

Chapter 5. The Humor of Relatability

Relatability is great for humor because it emphasizes a shared experience. When you can tap into those experiences, you can make statements and jokes that have lasting power because people will immediately understand your meaning.

Chapter 6. Emphasizing Contrast

Contrast and defied expectations are foundations of humor because they lull people into a sense of security, only to breach it immediately after.

Chapter 7. False Importance

Reacting in unexpected ways to normal, run of the mill events or statements can create humor because you are shaking people out of their normal routine and giving them something to think about in a funny way.

Chapter 8. Vivid and Outlandish Imagery

Our daily vocabulary and sense of description is sorely lacking. The first step to being funny is to do so in an understated way. Start to think in more vivid and creative words and phrases and the rest will start to follow naturally.

Chapter 9. The Art of Misconstruing

Misconstruing is the easiest way to initiate a joke with people, or get people out of a topic that you have no interest in. You just make an assumption, or pretend to play dumb, and suddenly you are in another topic altogether without any transition needed.

Chapter 10. The Power of Irony

Irony is essentially when you say two things at once, and it is up to the listener to deduce which is your true sentiment. You can use this slight moment of ambiguity to your advantage through ironic simile, ironic statements, and elements of sarcasm.

Chapter 11. Instigate a Banter Chain

A banter chain sounds like improv comedy. You are creating the chain with the other person and actively collaborating to build it up. All you have to do is agree with them, amplify their sentiment, and go with the flow.

Chapter 12. Skip the Middle Step

Skipping the middle step takes the action out of the traditional three step joke structure, and makes a plain statement funny because of what is implied.

Chapter 13. The Six Questions Approach

When you know the parameters and expectations of any circumstance, you can then alter one or two of those elements to see how it changes the circumstance drastically with humorous results. The six questions are the classic journalist's questions, so this approach helps you get better with gathering information about people and situations in general.

Chapter 14. Instant Role Play

Role play is predicated on actively assigning someone a role, and the role is something that is relative to you. When you put them into the role, you give yourself a role relative to that in status or ability, and then you stay in character and ask questions to encourage them to as well.

Chapter 15. The Comic Triple

The comic triple is one of the most famous joke structures. It gives a two-part setup, and then the third part of the triple completely shatters expectations. An easier way of thinking about this is to just state two positives, then one negative about something.

Chapter 16. Sarcasm? No way.

Sarcasm is truly the art of saying something without saying it at all. In fact, you are saying the opposite of what you feel and relying on other people to deduce your true meaning based on everything besides your actual words.

Chapter 17. The Witty Comeback Machine

Witty comebacks are easy because you can make them formulaic to a degree. Agree and bounce it back to the other person, which also has the benefit of making you look secure and comfortable with your identity.

Chapter 18. Five Quick Comic Quips

Some quick comic quips you can utilize are schadenfreude, acknowledging the elephant in the room, literally stating what you see, misdirection, and reactionary humor.